Entrepreneur®
MAGAZINE'S

startup

Start Your Own

WHOLESALE DISTRIBUTION BUSINESS

Your Step-by-Step Guide to Succ

Bridget McCrea

EP
Entrepreneur.
Press

Editorial Director: Jere L. Calmes
Managing Editor: Marla Markman
Cover Design: Beth Hansen-Winter
Production: Eliot House Productions
Composition: Armstrong Brown Design

This publication is designed to provide accurate and authoritative information in regard to the subject matter covered. It is sold with the understanding that the publisher is not engaged in rendering legal, accounting or other professional services. If legal advice or other expert assistance is required, the services of a competent professional person should be sought.

Library of Congress Cataloging-in-Publication Data
McCrea, Bridget.
    Start your own wholesale distribution business/by Bridget McCrea.
      p.   cm.   —(Entrepreneur magazine's start up)
    Includes bibliographical references and index.
    ISBN 1-891984-94-2
      1. Wholesale trade. 2. Entrepreneurship. I. Title. II. Series.

    HF5420.M33 2003
    658.8'6'0681—dc21   2003054959

Printed in Canada

09 08 07 06 05 04 03   10 9 8 7 6 5 4 3 2 1

Contents

▲

Preface

Thinking back to my first "real job," I remember walking into the small showroom full of welding supplies and miscellaneous products hanging on pegs and wondering to myself, "What in the world does this company do?"

At the time, all I knew about a welding supply distributorship was that it paid well compared to the rest of the jobs I had interviewed for, and the owner seemed slightly impressed with my resume. With that, I found myself in the position of office manager for a three-person wholesale distributorship. My duties included loading up trucks bound for job

▲

sites with cylinders of welding gases, packing and shipping boxes of welding wire headed overseas to companies like Air Products, and delivering damaged hydraulic gauges to a repair shop for a local cryogenics plant.

What followed was four years of hands-on experience in the wholesale distribution business. When I became a business writer, that job experience stuck, and I landed various distribution and industry-related assignments.

Today, the distribution landscape is a bit different than it was back in the early '90s when I was filling out government bids for welding machines. Rumors are running rampant, and buzzwords such as *disintermediation*, *the Internet*, and *direct sales* are being tossed around like crazy. On the surface, they appear to threaten the very existence of the wholesale distribution industry. Deep down, however, it's a different story.

The fact is, manufacturers couldn't survive without distribution networks. For example, I recently interviewed a large Sweden-based bearings manufacturer for *Industrial Distribution* magazine. More than once during the interview, the company's spokesperson mentioned that the manufacturer is "highly dependent" on its worldwide team of 8,000 industrial distributors. In fact, the company is so dependent on them that it just developed a Web site for all its distributors to use not only for online commerce, but also as an information source.

On the other side of the coin, the companies and other organizations that buy from distributors are also highly dependent on these expert middlemen. No manufacturer in the world can give the proper amount of attention to every end user. However, when territories are broken down and covered by individual distributorships, the task suddenly becomes more manageable. Take the contractor stuck on a job site in need of technical assistance with a product just purchased through a local distributor. Who do you think he should call—the distributor or the manufacturer? One is local, while the other will probably require a long-distance call and some time spent on hold, probably from a cellular phone.

In the end, it doesn't look like the wholesale distribution industry is going to be disintermediated (i.e., phased out by direct sellers and buyers who no longer want to deal with a middleman) anytime soon. In fact, the industry is doing quite well, as you'll read in this book. Plus, manufacturers will always rely on distributors to act on their behalf when it comes to functions such as customer service, sales, collections, and marketing.

After meeting all the entrepreneurs and experts we interviewed during the research phase of this book, you'll see that the wholesale distribution sector is actually thriving nicely. Good luck in your ventures, and I hope this book assists you in realizing your dreams of entrepreneurship.

1

Introduction
to Wholesale
Distribution

So you want to start a wholesale distributorship. Whether you're currently a white-collar professional, a manager worried about being downsized, or bored with your current job, this might be the right business for you. Much like the merchant traders of the 18th century, you'll be trading goods for profit. And while the romantic notion of standing on

a dock in the dead of night haggling over a tea shipment may be a bit far-fetched, the modern-day wholesale distributor evolved from those hardy traders who bought and sold goods hundreds of years ago.

The Distributor's Role

As you probably know, manufacturers produce products and retailers sell them to end users. A can of motor oil, for example, is manufactured and packaged, then sold to automobile owners through retail outlets and/or repair shops. In between, however, there are a few key operators—also known as distributors—that serve to move the product from manufacturer to market. Some are retail distributors, the kind that sell directly to consumers (end users). Others are known as merchant wholesale distributors; they buy products from the manufacturer or other source, then move them from their warehouses to companies that want to either resell the products to end users or use them in their own operations.

According to *U.S. Industry and Trade Outlook*, a yearly publication issued by The McGraw-Hill Companies and the U.S. Department of Commerce/International Trade Administration, wholesale trade includes establishments that sell products to retailers; merchants; contractors; and/or industrial, institutional, and commercial users. Wholesale distribution firms, which sell both durable goods (furniture, office equipment, industrial supplies, and other goods that can be used repeatedly) and non-durable goods (printing and writing paper, groceries, chemicals, and periodicals), don't sell to ultimate household consumers.

Three types of operation can perform the functions of wholesale trade: wholesale distributors; manufacturers' sales branches and offices; and agents, brokers, and commission agents. As a wholesale distributor, you will probably run an independently owned and operated firm that buys and sells products of which you have taken ownership. Generally, such operations are run from one or more warehouses where inventory goods are received and later shipped to customers.

Put simply, as the owner of a wholesale distributorship, you will be buying goods to sell at a profit, much like a retailer would. The only difference is that you'll be working in a business-to-business realm by selling to retail companies and other wholesale firms like your own, and not to the buying public. This is, however, somewhat of a traditional definition. For example, companies such as Sam's Club and BJ's Warehouse have been using warehouse membership clubs, where consumers are able to buy at what appear to be wholesale prices, for some time now, thus blurring the lines. However, the traditional wholesale distributor is still the one who buys "from the source" and sells to a reseller.

Getting Into the Game

Today, total wholesale trade sales are approximately $4.3 trillion, of which $2.6 trillion is booked by wholesale distributors. Since 1958 wholesale distributors' share of wholesale trade has increased steadily from 48 percent in 1958 to a recent 59 percent. That's a big chunk of money, and one that you can tap into with the help of this book.

The field of wholesale distribution is a true buying and selling game—one that requires good negotiation skills, a nose for sniffing out the next "hot" item in your particular category, and keen salesmanship. The idea is to buy the product at a low price, then make a profit by tacking on a dollar amount that still makes the deal attractive to your customer.

Experts agree that to succeed in the wholesale distribution business, an individual should possess a varied job background. Most experts feel a sales background is necessary, as are the "people skills" that go with being an outside salesperson who hits the streets and/or picks up the phone and goes on a cold-calling spree to search for new customers.

In addition to sales skills, the owner of a new wholesale distribution company will need the operational skills necessary for running such a company. For example, finance and business management skills and/or experience is necessary, as is the ability to handle the "back end" (those activities that go on behind the scenes, like warehouse setup and organization, shipping and receiving, customer service, etc.). Of course, these back-end functions can also be handled by employees with experience in these areas if your budget allows.

"Operating very efficiently and turning your inventory over quickly are the keys to making money," says Adam Fein, president of Pembroke Consulting Inc., a Philadelphia strategic consulting firm. "It's a service business that deals with business customers, as opposed to general consumers. The start-up entrepreneur must be able to understand customer needs and learn how to serve them well."

According to Fein, hundreds of new wholesale distribution businesses are started every year, typically by ex-salespeople from larger distributors who break out on their own with a few clients in tow. "Whether they can grow the firm and really become a long-term entity is the much more difficult guess," says Fein. "Success in wholesale distribution involves moving from a customer service/ sales orientation to the operational process of managing a very complex business." Luckily, the book in your hands will help take the guesswork out of this transition by giving you the tools you need to succeed.

Beware!
Remember that as a wholesale distributor, your customers have their own customers to satisfy. Because of this, they have more at stake than the typical customer who is shopping at a discount distributor that serves mainstream consumers.

Setting Up Shop

When it comes to setting up shop, your needs will vary according to what type of product you choose to specialize in. Someone could conceivably run a successful wholesale distribution business from their basement, but storage needs would eventually hamper the company's success. "If you're running a distribution company from home, then you're much more of a broker than a distributor," says Fein, noting that while a distributor takes title and legal ownership of the products, a broker simply facilitates the transfer of products. "However, through the use of the Internet, there are some very interesting alternatives to becoming a distributor [who takes] physical possession of the product." (Read more about using the Internet in your operations in Chapter 10 of this book.)

According to Fein, wholesale distribution companies are frequently started in areas where land is not too expensive, and where buying or renting warehouse space is affordable. "Generally, wholesale distributors are not located in downtown shopping areas, but off the beaten path," says Fein. "If, for example, you're serving building or electrical contractors, you'll need to choose a location in close proximity to them in order to be accessible as they go about their jobs."

Finding Your Niche

Upon opening the doors of your wholesale distribution business, you will certainly find yourself in good company. To date, there are approximately 300,000 distributors in the United States, representing $2.6 trillion in annual revenues. Wholesale distribution contributes 16 percent to the value of the nation's gross domestic product (GDP), and most distribution channels are still highly fragmented and comprise many small, privately held companies. "My research shows that there are only 2,000 distributors in the United States with revenues greater than $100 million," comments Fein.

And that's not all: Every year, U.S. retail cash registers ring up about $2.7 trillion in sales, and of that, about a quarter comes from general merchandise, apparel, and furniture (GAF) sales. This is a positive for wholesale distributors, who rely heavily on retailers as customers. To measure the scope of GAF, try to imagine every consumer item sold; then remove the cars, building materials, and food. The rest, including computers, clothing, sports equipment, and other items, falls into the GAF total. Such goods come directly from manufacturers or through wholesalers and brokers. Then they are retailed in department, high-volume, and specialty stores—all of which will make up your client base once you open the doors of your wholesale distribution firm.

All this is good news for the start-up entrepreneur looking to launch a wholesale distribution company. However, there are a few dangers you should be aware of. For starters, consolidation is rampant in this industry. Some sectors are contracting more quickly than others. For example, pharmaceutical wholesaling has consolidated more than just about any other sector, according to Fein. Since 1975 mergers and acquisitions have reduced the number of U.S. companies in that sector from 200 to about 50. And the largest four companies control more than 80 percent of the distribution market.

To combat the consolidation trend, many independent distributors are turning to the specialty market. "Many entrepreneurs are finding success by picking up the golden crumbs that are left on the table by the national companies," Fein says. "As distribution has evolved from a local to a regional to a national business, the national companies [can't or don't want to] cost-effectively service certain types of customers. Often, small customers get left behind or are just not [profitable] for the large distributors to serve."

In addition to consolidating, the wholesale distribution industry is evolving rapidly, which translates to both positive and negative changes. For instance, as discussed in the Preface of this book, there are implications of disintermediation trends across various industries. Several years ago, strategists and futurists began predicting

Beware!
Consolidation is running rampant in many industries. Before choosing your niche, do some market research on your customer base (especially if you're going to limit yourself to a particular region) to be sure those customers aren't ripe for consolidation. If they are, you could see your client base shrink quickly.

that companies would increasingly sell directly to consumers, cutting out distributors and any other distribution intermediaries, including some retailers. The predicted change was given a fancy term: disintermediation. It has yet to happen, but the threat persists as an increasing number of manufacturers and end users find one another directly. However, no matter what changes may be in store, smart wholesale distributors will always find a way to adapt.

The Technological Edge

Today, more than 170 million people around the world have access to the Internet. This is good news for the wholesale distributor who is willing to be flexible in the information age. While traditional players may be threatened by the Internet as a new sales channel, a start-up will be more apt to take technology by the horns and use it to its advantage.

As e-commerce has evolved into more than just a business opportunity, traditional "brick and mortar" businesses are no longer able to rely on traditional forms of selling products to their customers. Product distribution and delivery trends are being impacted as the Internet becomes the "new way" of doing business. They must also be available to their customers via the Internet. For this reason, wholesale distributors—like their vendors—must be willing to test the waters of this new medium. Some are doing it by setting up their own informational Web sites; others list their companies and offerings on mall-type sites that are devoted to wholesale distributors; and still others are creating e-commerce-enabled sites where customers can buy directly through the Web.

E-commerce, or the process of buying and selling via the Internet, is undoubtedly a major consideration for all wholesale distributors. The Gartner Group, an information technology advisory firm in Stamford, Connecticut, has outlined two possible scenarios to describe how the Internet could negatively affect wholesalers:

> **Bright Idea**
>
> You can take a trip on the information superhighway to visit a few of your potential competitors. Key the words "wholesale distributor" into your favorite search engine, or narrow it down geographically by adding your city and/or state to the search string.

1. Manufacturers post products on the Internet by using a bulletin board system, thus letting customers search the source globally by using online search engines.
2. Manufacturers use the Internet to gain direct access to customers, thus bypassing the wholesale distributor altogether.

As with fighting the trend toward consolidation, a smart wholesaler can combat both of these scenarios with a bit of ingenuity and creativity. Finding a unique niche

Ride the High-Tech Wave

It's no secret that technology has become a major force in the world, so why not try your hand at reselling computers and related equipment? While some computer manufacturers, such as Gateway and Dell, prefer to sell direct to the consumer, many others rely on the wholesale distribution channel to get their products to market. And the numbers look good: Investments in computing and telecommunications equipment by American corporations have risen from 29 percent to 53 percent over the past decade, according to the U.S. Department of Commerce.

In a recent report, Commerce Secretary William M. Daley expressed optimism for the nation's economy and said that more than 80 percent of the manufacturing industries and all of the major service sectors are expected to grow well into the new millennium. Leading the way, he says, is the information technology sector, which grew by 8 percent in 1999 alone.

is one sharp move, whether it's serving a group of consumers that manufacturers or larger distributors can't be bothered with, or perhaps buying in bulk quantities and then selling broken-down quantities to smaller firms that don't want to make big inventory investments.

Including value-added services can also give you a competitive edge. These include (but are not limited to) simplifying the transfer of product, helping smooth out possible glitches in the information flow, and making transfer of payment easier. In other words, rather than going directly to the manufacturer—who is often more concerned with producing the hard goods than dealing with customer needs—retailers and other distributors can deal with a wholesaler who specializes in customer needs. Wholesalers can also make themselves valuable by keeping goods on hand for customers who would otherwise have to deal with long lead times when buying direct. "That availability very often makes the wholesale distributor a backup for, and extension of, the customer's own inventory system," says Fein. And e-commerce itself can be a boon to

Beware!

If you're planning to start a wholesale distribution business from home, check with your local zoning board about the legality of shipping and receiving merchandise at your home. For example, many cities do not allow the delivery of goods from vehicles such as tractor trailers in residential neighborhoods.

the wholesale distributor, especially when it comes to finding new customers and hunting down new product manufacturers and vendors from which to buy.

Getting Started

For entrepreneurs looking to start their own wholesale distributorship, there are basically three avenues to choose from: buy an existing business, start from scratch, or buy into a business opportunity.

Buying an existing business can be costly and might even be risky, depending on the level of success and reputation of the distributorship you want to buy. The positive side of buying a business is that you can probably tap into the seller's knowledge bank, and you may even inherit his or her existing client base, which could prove extremely valuable.

The second option, starting from scratch, can also be costly, but it allows for a true "make or break it yourself" scenario that is guaranteed not to be preceded by an existing owner's reputation. On the downside, you will be building a reputation from scratch, which means lots of sales and marketing for at least the first two years, or until your client base is large enough to reach critical mass.

The last option is perhaps the most risky, as all business opportunities must be thoroughly explored before any money or precious time is invested. However, the right opportunity can mean support, training, and quick success if the originating company has already proven itself to be profitable, reputable, and durable.

Dollar Stretcher

To avoid spending excess money during the start-up phase, list everything you think you need and then ask yourself: Why do I need this item? How will it help me be more productive? Can I do without it for six months or a year while my business is getting started? Do this for every purchase and you'll avoid the urge to spend on impulse items.

Regardless of which avenue you choose, a new distributorship will require a few key pieces of equipment to get started. In the office, a personal computer, several phone lines, a fax machine, and access to a reliable shipping method will all be necessary. Most wholesalers drop-ship their products through the use of shipping services (UPS, Airborne, Federal Express, etc.), though some who deliver to their local areas use their own leased or purchased delivery vehicles. In the end, it truly depends on the product, lead times, and proximity of your customer base. With the exception of the entrepreneur who is wholesaling T-shirts from his or her basement, a generous amount of warehouse space will be necessary, as will a location that is in close proximity to your customers.

During the start-up process, you'll also need to assess your own financial situation and decide if you're going to start your business on a full- or part-time basis. A full-time commitment probably means quicker success, namely because you will be devoting all of your time to the new company's success.

Because the amount of start-up capital necessary will be highly dependent on what you choose to sell, the numbers vary. For instance, an Ohio-based wholesale distributor of men's ties and belts started his company with $700 worth of closeout ties bought from the manufacturer, and a few basic pieces of office equipment. At the higher end of the spectrum, a Virginia-based distributor of fine wines started with $1.5 million used mainly for inventory, a large warehouse, internal necessities (pallet racking, pallets, forklift), and a few Chevrolet Astro vans for delivery.

According to Mark Dierolf, president of Gilbertsville, Pennsylvania-based consulting firm Innovative Distribution Solutions Inc., the average wholesale distributor will need to be in business three to five years to be profitable. There are exceptions, of course. Take, for example, the ambitious entrepreneur who sets up his garage as a warehouse to stock full of small hand tools. Using his own vehicle

Industry at a Glance

This trend report indicates the number of U.S. wholesale distribution companies, by company size, for the eight-year period from 1992–1999 in the SIC code range: 5,000–5,199.

	1 to 9	10 to 19	20 to 49	50 to 99	100 to 499	500 to 999	1,000 or more	Total Companies	Total Employees
Total 1992	486,732	76,366	44,172	11,483	6,139	345	152	625,389	6,404,743
Total 1993	524,351	76,371	43,703	11,284	6,105	320	144	662,278	6,354,109
Total 1994	581,763	75,943	43,486	11,149	6,155	304	149	718,949	6,547,553
Total 1995	572,087	75,719	44,028	11,305	6,232	304	148	709,823	6,564,287
Total 1996	551,596	74,567	43,394	11,223	6,175	301	130	687,386	6,338,918
Total 1997	502,523	66,723	39,371	10,332	5,760	285	124	625,118	5,783,284
Total 1998	556,346	74,846	44,751	11,916	6,758	338	156	695,111	6,572,421
Total 1999	528,831	75,494	45,193	12,167	6,874	383	165	669,107	6,632,533
% Change 1992–99	+9%	-1%	+2%	+6%	+12%	-10%	+8%	+7%	+4%

Source: Industrial Market Information Inc.

and relying on the low overhead that his home provides, he could conceivably start making money within 6 to 12 months, according to Dierolf.

"Wholesale distribution is a very large segment of the economy and constitutes about 6 percent of the nation's GDP," says Pembroke Consulting Inc.'s Fein. "That said, there are many different subsegments and industries within the realm of wholesale distribution, and some offer much greater opportunities than others."

Among those subsegments are wholesale distributors that specialize in a unique niche (e.g., the distributor that sells specialty foods to grocery stores), larger distributors that sell everything from soup to nuts (e.g., the distributor with warehouses nationwide and a large stock of various, unrelated closeout items), and midsized distributors who choose an industry (hand tools, for example) and offer a variety of products to myriad customers.

Regardless of which subsegment you choose, this book will give you the information you need to realize your dreams of owning a wholesale distribution business. In the next chapter, we'll examine the operational aspect of owning a wholesale distribution business.

Operations

Now that you have the "big picture" view of the wholesale distribution business, and now that you know your potential for success as a start-up business owner, we'll give you the lowdown on just how your new company will operate.

A wholesale distributor's initial steps when venturing into the entrepreneurial landscape include defining a customer base and locating reliable sources of product. The latter will soon become commonly known as your "vendors" or "suppliers."

There are, of course, myriad other start-up considerations that we'll discuss in this book. The cornerstone of every distribution cycle, however, is the basic flow of product from manufacturer to distributor to customer. As a wholesale distributor, your task in the equation will involve matching up the manufacturer and customer by obtaining quality products at a reasonable price and then selling them to the companies that need them.

In its simplest form, distribution simply means purchasing a product from a source—usually a manufacturer, but sometimes another distributor—and selling it to your customer. As a wholesale distributor, you will specialize in selling to customers—and even other distributors—who are in the business of selling to end users (usually the general public). It's one of the purest examples of the business-to-business function, as opposed to a business-to-consumer function, in which companies sell to the general public.

Weighing It Out: Operating Costs

No two distribution companies are alike, and each has its own unique needs. The entrepreneur who is selling closeout T-shirts from his basement, for example, has very different start-up financial needs than the one selling power tools from a warehouse in the middle of an industrial park.

Regardless of where a distributor sets up shop (read more about where to establish your company in Chapter 6 of this book), some basic operating costs apply across the board. For starters, necessities such as office space, a telephone, fax machine, and personal computer will make up the core of your business. (Read more about specialized equipment necessary for wholesale distributors in Chapter 7.) This means an office rental fee if you're working from anywhere but home, a telephone bill and ISP (Internet service provider) fees for getting on the Internet. (Find out more about standard office equipment in Chapter 7 of this book.)

No matter what type of products you plan to carry, you'll need some type of warehouse or storage space in which to store them; this means a leasing fee. Remember that if you lease a warehouse that has room for office space, you can combine both on one bill. If you're delivering locally, you'll also need an adequate vehicle to get around in. If your customer base is located farther than 40 miles from your home base, then you'll also need to set up a working relationship with one or more shipping companies such as UPS, Federal Express, or the U.S. Postal Service. Most distributors serve a mixed client base; some of the merchandise you move can be delivered via truck, while some will require shipping services. (Read more about whether you should lease

Dollar Stretcher

Even if you absolutely need to lease warehouse space, remember that you can still handle operations from a home-based office. Not only will this allow for 24-hour access to your nascent firm (sometimes a necessity in the "getting started" phase of business), but it will also allow you to write off a portion of your home for tax purposes.

or buy your vehicles in Chapter 7 of this book.)

While they may sound a bit overwhelming, the above necessities don't always have to be expensive—especially not during the start-up phase. For example, Keith S., owner of a wholesale tie and belt distributorship in Wickliffe, Ohio, started his distributorship from a corner of his living room. With no equipment other than a phone, fax machine, and computer, he grew his company from the living room to the basement to the garage and then into a shared warehouse space (the entire process took five years).

To avoid liability early on in his entrepreneurial venture, Keith rented pallet space in someone else's warehouse, where he stored his closeout ties and belts. This meant lower overhead for the entrepreneur, along with no utility bills, leases, or costly insurance policies in his name. In fact, it wasn't until he penned a deal with a Michigan distributor for a large project that he had to store product and relabel the closeout ties with his firm's own insignia. As a result, he finally rented a 1,000-square-foot warehouse space. But even that was shared, this time with another Ohio distributor. "I don't believe in having any liability if I don't have to have it," he says. "A warehouse is a liability."

Whether you choose to store product in your hall closet or in a 10,000-square-foot warehouse is highly dependent on your budget and on the size of the products you're distributing. Either way, this book will help you figure out what will work best. (You can read more about where to locate your company and inventory in Chapter 6 of this book.)

The Day-to-Day Routine

Like many other businesses, wholesale distributors perform functions such as sales and marketing, accounting, shipping and receiving, and customer service on a daily basis. They also handle tasks such as contacting existing and prospective customers, processing orders, supporting customers who need help with problems that may crop up, and doing market research (for example, who better than the "in the trenches" distributor to find out if a manufacturer's new product will be viable in a particular market?).

"One reason that wholesale distributors have increased their share of total wholesale sales is that they can perform these functions more effectively and efficiently than

Smart Tip

Tip...

Executive suites are a great way to partner with other small-business owners, limit your liability and share resources such as secretaries and fax machines. Check out the "Executive Suites" section of your local Yellow Pages for one in your area.

manufacturers or customers," comments Adam Fein of Philadelphia-based Pembroke Consulting Inc.

To handle all of these tasks and whatever else may come their way during the course of the day, most distributors rely on specialized software packages that tackle such functions as inventory control, shipping and receiving, accounting, client management, and bar-coding (the application of computerized UPC codes to track inventory). (Read more about specialized software and technological requirements for distributors in Chapter 7 of this book.)

The Distributor's Daily Checklist

Without a daily agenda, who knows if you're actually completing all the tasks that need to be done? Try using the following checklist as a guide when going through your day-to-day activities:

❑ Check phone messages, incoming faxes, and e-mail messages from the night before (especially if you're dealing with customers in other states or countries; they may have quitting times that are later than yours).

❑ If any of those messages were product orders, confirm them with the customers (if necessary) and place the orders with the appropriate vendors.

❑ Review the day's delivery and/or shipping schedule. If you're delivering to a local area, be sure to call all nearby customers to see if they need anything while you're in the area.

❑ Set up a sales call contact sheet (see page 17 for an example) and set a reasonable goal for how many new customers your efforts should net each week.

❑ Follow up with vendors on any deliveries you're expecting, or any that may be overdue.

❑ Handle any internal functions that may need attention: hiring or firing employees, accounting and bookkeeping, financial projections, etc.

❑ Arrange for any late-day shipments (if applicable) to customers who may have called in for emergency deliveries.

❑ Prepare delivery schedule for the following day.

And while not all distributors have adopted the high-tech way of doing business, Dave Spreen, branch manager for Tom Duffy Co., a Eureka, California, wholesale flooring distributor, says those who have embraced technology are definitely benefiting from their forward-thinking ways. "For us, creating greater efficiencies of operations has been the challenge, but also a catalyst for growth," he says. "We adopted a new computer system in 1990, and it definitely facilitated our success."

Spreen adds that when Tom Duffy Co. identified the areas of the company's operations that were most in need of improvement (e.g., inventory control), it eventually led to efficiencies that boosted the firm's bottom line.

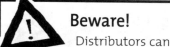

Beware!

Distributors can fall into the rut of offering customers only products that they've already purchased. Don't let this happen to you. Instead, make customers special offers, tell them about new product offerings, and introduce them to products that they may have never considered. A little customer education goes a long way, so keep them informed!

Tracking Your Efforts

There's no room for complacency in business, and the wholesale distributor who contacts both existing and potential customers on a regular basis gains an edge over competitors who may not be so diligent. Sometimes, you may even get a sale just by being there at the right time. In other words, the customer on the other end of the phone would have bought those 12 cases of masking tape from another distributor if you hadn't called at the right moment and told him you'd be in his area the next morning.

Smart Tip

Even though your business is just starting up, you should avoid the Rolodex and use a computer-based database system to track clients and business partners. Eventually, you'll want to do this anyway, so get in the habit of using the electronic version now, and you'll be ahead of the game.

To keep track of whom you call, what you offer them, and when you should call again, use a call log. This can be done via a contact management database such as ACT!, Microsoft Outlook, or any number of titles available at a local software store or on the Internet. Another option is to do it the old-fashioned way (which might be necessary at first) and just keep a written log using multiple sales call contact sheets (see page 17).

As your customer base grows, you may need to add more categories to your sales call contact sheet. Be flexible, and remember to always make extra offers to your customers. It

Bright Idea

When pitching your offerings to new customers, bring along comparison figures that show how much they can save by buying from you in smaller, more digestible quantities. For example, you might let them know that you're passing on a 5 percent discount to them thanks to your ability to buy in larger quantities at wholesale prices.

may be weeks until they decide to take you up on the offer, but customers will always appreciate your willingness to introduce them to new products.

Staying on Top of an Evolving Industry

With threats of direct selling (when the manufacturer sells to the end user or other customer instead of using a distributor), the Internet, industry consolidation, and disintermediation (the elimination of the middleman in the sales process) looming, distributors appear to be facing an uncertain future. However, there will always be a need for the entrepreneur who can provide services and support that a manufacturer simply doesn't have the time or resources to offer.

In other words, successful distributors in today's rapidly evolving business landscape will be those who think beyond the product to other value-added services they can provide. For example, a small grocery store may sell only 20 flashlights annually. In such a situation, buying direct from the manufacturer would hardly be feasible, since most manufacturers sell in large quantities (known as "lots"). That's where the distributor comes in: By purchasing 2,000 of the flashlights and then selling them to their customers (in this case, retailers who sell to the general public), the distributor is fulfilling a true need. Not only is the customer able to save money by purchasing from someone who bought an entire lot of the product, but they can avoid stocking 2,000 flashlights on their shelves for an inordinate amount of time.

And while customers obviously benefit from the distributor's ability to break down large quantities, manufacturers also benefit. The size of a wholesale distributor's purchase serves a valuable function by satisfying the manufacturer's need for efficiency, namely because they can manufacture and ship in large quantities, as opposed to smaller lots. It's a true win-win-win situation for all three parties, and it's one all wholesale distributors should work to maximize as they progress in business.

In the next chapter, we'll discuss how to stay ahead of the curve by researching your market, defining who your customers are and concentrating on those who will bring your company the most profits.

Sales Call Contact Sheet

Customer name: _____

Company name: _____

Address: _____

Phone number: _____

Products frequently purchased: _____

Possible cross-sells and upsells: _____

CALLS

Date: _____

Time: _____

Contact's name: _____

Purchases: _____

Delivery date: _____

Additional products offered: _____

_____

Notes: _____

_____

_____

_____

_____

Defining
and Researching
Your Market

Because every company relies on a pool of customers to sell its products and/or services to, the next logical step in the start-up process involves defining exactly who will be included in that pool. Defining this group early on will allow you to develop business strategies, develop your mission or answer the question "why am I in business?," and tailor your operations to meet the needs of your customer base.

As a wholesale distributor, your choice of customers includes the following:

- *Retail businesses.* This includes establishments such as grocery stores, independent retail stores, large department stores, and power retailers like Wal-Mart and Target.

- *Retail distributors.* This includes the distributors who sell to those retailers that you may find impenetrable on your own. For example, if you can't "get in" at a power retailer like Wal-Mart, you may be able to sell to one of its distributors.

- *Exporters.* These are companies that collect United States–manufactured goods and ship them overseas.

- *Other wholesale distributors.* It's always best to buy from the source, but that isn't always possible, due to exclusive contracts and issues like one-time needs (e.g., a distributor who needs ten hard hats for a customer who is particular about buying one brand). For this reason, wholesale distributors often find themselves selling to other distributors.

> **Smart Tip** Tip...
>
> Before bidding on a government project, read the fine print on the RFP (request for proposal). Often government orders require special packaging and shipping that can inflate your costs for processing and shipping the order.

In addition, Uncle Sam is always looking for items that wholesale distributors sell. In fact, for wholesale distributors, selling to the government presents a great opportunity. For the most part, it's a matter of filling out the appropriate forms and getting on a "bid list." After you become an official government supplier, the various buying agencies will either fax or e-mail you requests for bids for materials needed by schools, various agencies, shipyards, and other facilities. "For a small wholesale distributor, there are some great advantages to selling to the government," says Mark Dierolf of Gilbertsville, Pennsylvania-based Innovative Distribution Solutions Inc. "They typically have the opportunity to win those contracts because bigger companies don't want them. In fact, it poses a wonderful opportunity for the small distributor."

Market Research Tactics

To reach customers other than the government (which tends to act as a captive audience that you can deal with on a separate basis from the rest of your customer pool), you will first need to do some basic market research. Done properly, this will aid in the establishment of your wholesale distribution business and will help you be better prepared before opening the doors to your company.

Market research for a business can run from a simple series of phone calls to very expensive and complex studies. Unfortunately, too many small businesses—wholesale distributors included—do little or no market research and end up missing out on valuable information concerning their customers' wants and needs. It's this information that can not only increase sales, but also help you avoid making major mistakes during the early stages of business.

> **Bright Idea**
>
> If you're afraid that your market research surveys will be ignored or delayed, try offering a perk that will motivate your recipients to share their views with you. For example, you might try offering 10 percent off of the recipient's first purchase in exchange for returning the survey by a certain date.

One of the cornerstones of market research is determining customer needs in the marketplace. This research is conducted with both current (if applicable) and targeted customers. By using a well-thought-out market research plan, you will uncover what is driving your customers' companies, what their needs are, and what features they're seeking in the products and services you plan to offer. This information will also help you determine the market potential for a product or service, including what kind of demand already exists for the product, and what price customers are willing to pay.

Once your company is established, you will also want to do market research that assesses current customer satisfaction. Wholesale distributors must stay abreast of issues such as whether or not they are serving their current customers well. Through effective market research, problems can be corrected, new products or services can be developed, and a closer relationship can be fostered with existing customers.

Online Surveys

Over the next few years, it is expected that seven out of 10 Americans and 1.5 billion people worldwide will be online—all of them a few clicks and a couple of keystrokes away from your new business. Why not take advantage of this huge audience by conducting online market research surveys?

For the wholesale distributor, online surveys can be a true godsend. They are relatively inexpensive to produce, costing as little as $1 for a ten-question survey. They are also fast, targeted, innovative, and accurate. Currently, there are several sources online that produce and analyze such surveys (e.g., Compusurvey at www.compusurvey.com and Survey Site at www.surveysite2.com). Or you might choose to do the surveys yourself if you have a viable list of recipients to whom you can send them, and extra hands to do the tabulating. Surveybuilder.com, Question

Builder.com, and Greenfield Online (www. greenfieldonline.com) allow you to produce and send ten-question surveys for an average cost of about $1 apiece. Archiving, tabulating, and comparing results costs extra, depending on your needs.

To get started, simply key the words "online market research" into your favorite search engine. From there, pick a few companies, ask for and check references, and then do a test run based on your needs. You may be surprised at how fast and efficient it is to do market research online.

Dollar Stretcher

If your budget doesn't allow for the hiring of a market research firm, and if your time is too limited to do the market research on your own, try tapping into one or more of the publications, associations, and professional organizations listed in the Appendix of this book. Some organizations compile and distribute industry-specific market research data to members, often at no cost.

Going Straight to the Source

Paul Lineback, vice president and general manager of Pyramid Products, a Spokane, Washington-based distributor of golf ball displays, says his company did most of its market research right at the source: the pro shops to which the company intended to sell product. Some were right on the golf courses; others were located in strip malls and shopping centers. All proved helpful in determining the viability of the wholesale distributor's product.

"By going directly to them, and to trade shows and the Internet, we found it pretty easy to pin down our market," he says. And while he says he didn't use any surveys, the one question he and his team asked was: Would this product I'm selling be marketable and viable in this market? "We talked to some of our competitors as well, just to get a feel for what the marketplace would be," adds Lineback.

According to Adam Fein of Philadelphia-based Pembroke Consulting Inc., new wholesale distribution businesses have two general issues to consider during the market research phase. They are:

1. Will the industry channel continue to be viable? According to Fein, the Internet is currently restructuring many distribution channels. Those thinking of starting a wholesale distribution business should first ensure that their company will actually provide high value to their customers. This is necessary because wholesale distributors are finding themselves being disintermediated, or cut out of the channel, by manufacturers who choose to sell directly to customers and customers who choose to buy directly from manufacturers. (See Chapter 2 for more discussion on disintermediation and how smart wholesale distributors are overcoming this challenge.)

Getting to Know You

Before trying to figure out just what will make potential customers open their wallets and start buying from your new wholesale distributorship, ask them the following questions:

- ◯ How often do you buy products from wholesale distributors?
- ◯ What are the three products you purchase most often from wholesale distributors?
- ◯ If a new wholesale distributor of (fill in the blank with your offerings) in (your city and state) were to open, would you consider using it as a new source of products?
- ◯ How satisfied are you with the service you're currently getting from your distributor of (fill in the blank with your offerings)?
- ◯ What is the number one thing you expect from a distributor?
- ◯ Do you feel you're currently getting that from your distributor of (fill in the blank with your offerings)?
- ◯ What are the top three things you'd like to see from a new distributor?

2. What competitors are currently in the market? Some distribution industries are very fragmented, meaning that they're made up of thousands of small, privately held companies. According to Fein, such companies tend to come and go because of challenges being posed to new companies opening up in the industry. On the other hand, some distribution industries have become highly consolidated and are dominated by large, national corporations. As a result, he says, in consolidated industries there are fewer opportunities for a general service, broad-based wholesale distribution company but many opportunities for the niche or specialized distributor.

Beware!

Some online survey companies continually screen the same group of candidates. Before working with such a company, be sure to inquire about its recipient list, how the recipients are gathered and screened, and what the recipients' specific demographics are.

Check Out the Competition

As Fein points out, researching the competition is crucial. You'll want to take a regional, national, and international (if applicable) view of what is going on around you in distribution circles. If you're planning to offer products to a regional group of potential buyers, be sure that there isn't already a niche player in your area. You can find out whether there is by calling the buyers themselves (those who are purchasing product for retail stores, for example), and asking them from whom they are buying. Because most buyers are out to get the best possible deal and are eager to work with quality suppliers, most will gladly share this information with you.

Doing a bit of competitive intelligence (i.e., getting the lowdown on the competition) before you open your doors will go a long way. Here are a few "talking points" to discuss with distributors who are already in

Dollar Stretcher

The Internet is a great, cheap place where small businesses can gain competitive intelligence. Check out your industry's trade magazines and associations and then go to a press release site such as PR Newswire (www.prnewswire.com) or Business Wire (www.businesswire.com) to see what information your competitors are sharing with the rest of the world.

your market. (We're not saying all of them will give up the information in detail, but it's worth a shot!)

- In what products and services does your company specialize?
- How is the local market (or the national or international market, depending on your own strategy) in terms of customer loyalty and its willingness to try new sources of product and new products in general?
- What is the average markup of your products?
- Do you find that this markup is acceptable to customers, or do you find yourself negotiating on a regular basis?
- How long did it take for your company to become profitable? Were there any unusual variables that came into play (e.g., was the company spun off from an already-successful firm, thus leading to a quicker payoff)?
- Overall, what are your thoughts on a new business coming into the market to sell (fill in the blank with your products)?

Finding a Profitable Niche

Once you have done the necessary research on your soon-to-be customers and competitors, you will have a much better idea of what type of niche your new company can fill. Profitable niches in today's wholesale distribution arena include, but are certainly not limited to, reselling products that require some degree of education on the seller's part. Take, for example, the pencil analogy: Selling traditional pencils is easy, but selling mechanical pencils that require a specific technique—and a refill—takes smarts. In the latter situation, wholesale distributors come in extremely handy because they can educate the customer, who can then educate his own end user, about the benefits and operations of the mechanical pencil.

In other words, what matters is not so much what you sell, but how you sell it. There are profitable opportunities in every industry—from beauty supplies to hand tools, beverages to snack foods. No matter what they're selling, wholesale distributors are discovering ways to reaffirm their value to suppliers and customers by revealing the superior service they have to offer, as well as the cost-saving efficiencies created by those services. This mind-set opens up a wealth of opportunities to provide greater attention to the individual needs of customers, a chance to develop margin growth, and greater flexibility in product offerings and diversification of the business. Remember—it wasn't too long ago that many people thought corporate behemoths such as Sears and Home Depot would be the demise of the small contractor and the wholesale distributor. Yet to this day, they have not had a significant impact on either.

Smart Tip

You might choose to distribute products to a particular region, but you'll probably be propositioned by far-flung companies to ship product outside your area (especially with the advent of the Internet, which can make a company Web site available to the world with just a few keystrokes). Develop a company-wide plan for handling these types of situations.

Beware!

Distributors who put too many eggs in one basket by catering only to a select group of customers may find themselves empty-handed when their customer base suffers an economic downturn. For example, the agriculture industry recently had a particularly bad year, so distributors of tools used to make farming equipment were adversely affected. Be smart and keep an eye open for new places to sell product, and for economic trends that might affect your company down the road.

The whole trick, of course, is to find that niche and make it work for you. In wholesale distribution, a niche is a particular area where your company can most excel and prosper—be it selling tie-dyed T-shirts, roller bearings, or sneakers. While some entrepreneurs may find their niche in a diverse area (for example, closeout goods purchased from manufacturers), others may wish to specialize (unique barstools that will be sold to regional bars and pubs).

On the other side of the coin, too much product and geographical specialization can hamper success. Take the barstool example. Let's say you were going to go with this idea but that in six months you'd already sold as many barstools as you could to the customer base within a 50-mile radius of your location. At that point, you would want to diversify your offerings, perhaps adding other bar-related items such as dartboards, pool cues, and other types of chairs.

The decision is yours: You can go into the wholesale distribution arena with a full menu of goods or a limited selection. Usually, that decision will be based on your finances, the amount of time you'll be able to devote to the business, and the resources available to you. Regardless of the choices you make, remember that market research provides critical information that enables a business to successfully go to market, and wholesale distributors should do as much as they can—on an ongoing basis. It is better to do simple research routinely than to shell out a lot of money once on a big research information project that may quickly become outdated.

In the next chapter, we'll discuss several issues you'll have to consider before opening your doors, including choosing a business name, what type of business licenses are required, and the various professional services you may need during the start-up phase and beyond.

Structuring
Your Business

You've defined your market and determined the viability of your business idea. Now get ready to focus on a few important ingredients that go into running a successful business. Some issues will be decided at the outset and pretty much forgotten about while you concentrate on getting your company profitable (issues such as business structure, company

Photo ©PhotoDisc Inc.

name, and the necessary licenses). Other matters are constantly evolving (for example, business insurance and the use of outside professionals, both of which will change as your business grows). Read on for more information about structuring your wholesale distributorship for maximum success.

Choosing a Name That Fits

The world is littered with business names. Some leave an impression, others do not, and still others leave people wondering "What the heck does that company do?" Take a look at your competitors to find out what type of name will best fit your business. Because your goal is not to attract the mainstream public, you'll want to come up with a catchy moniker that befits a true business-to-business company.

"Stay away from initials while you're at it." So says Mark Dierolf of Innovative Distribution Solutions Inc. in Gilbertsville, Pennsylvania. Five years ago, he says, no companies in the industrial wholesale business had the letters "ID" in their names. Now everyone is using it, making it hard for customers to tell them apart. And while potential customers may be attracted to the "ID," the distributor who uses those initials is sure to have a hard time standing apart from the pack.

Dierolf adds that new wholesale distributors should avoid getting too creative with their names. "If customers can't link your name to your line of business, then you are probably not going to get a lot of business," he says. Simple names work best, and fancy logos don't work very well in the distribution business. "Instead, your name should somehow form your logo," says Dierolf. "That is a better way to go."

Distributors often rely on their primary product line, supplier, or geographical location to dictate their companies' names. For example, one successful Maryland-based distributor of safety supplies uses "Safeware Inc.," while a distributor in Massachusetts that specializes in fasteners has found success with "Atlantic Fasteners." Still others rely on the family names of their founders to help them cut through the clutter. "Orco Supply," a California-based building supply distributor, and "B.C. MacDonald," a cutting tool distributor in Missouri, have both found success with this strategy.

While Dierolf may advise new distributors to avoid getting creative with their names, some distributors still insist on making up clever names that they hope will leave an impact on their future customers.

Keith S., of the Ohio-based wholesale accessories distributorship, says his firm's name has changed three times since inception. "Each time, we changed it based on

> ### Smart Tip
> Make sure your company name clearly defines your business for several years into the future. Changing a company name—should you choose to diversify into a different business area in a few years—can be a costly, time-intensive proposition.

The Right Name at the Right Time

At one entrepreneur's distributorship, the company name "E-Fastener" was way ahead of its time when it was first conceived in 1977. Few distributors were online back then. "The Internet was still taking shape at the time," says the entrepreneur.

With IBM already involved with online commerce, the entrepreneur says it was just a matter of waiting for the rest of the world to catch up with the rapidly evolving Internet—and then sit back and reap the rewards. "We actually didn't realize what an excellent name it was at the time," he adds. "Now it's fairly clear that we made a good choice. In fact, we have all sorts of people trying to infringe on our name, and still others who have offered to buy it from us."

The entrepreneur adds that the business's name has done its part in attracting and retaining customers, and has been an attention-getter for his wholesale distribution business. Says the seasoned distributor, "It's probably the one thing that works best in the company."

what we were trying to accomplish in the sales department, and what image we needed to portray to our customers," he explains. "Our market concept is to develop a wide assortment of seasonal promotions that can be sold to the same customers," says Keith. "This gives us a reason to visit our customers every month and to give them a stronger reason to buy from us." For this reason, the firm's name works well.

Regardless of what route you take when naming your business—naming it after yourself, getting help from a marketing guru, or sticking with something that relates to your line of business—the key is to come up with something that will stick in your customers' minds as your wholesale distribution company grows, expands, and prospers.

Beware!

Don't let your mission statement corner you into doing business in an unprofitable manner. As your distributorship grows, remember that it may need to be tweaked to meet changing market demands, evolving customer needs and new opportunities. Sticking to your core values is always recommended, but don't let your mission statement make you miss out on a great opportunity.

On a Mission: Developing a Positioning Statement

Some business owners keep them in their heads, others write them down on scraps of paper, and still others put them in formal documents like business plans. Put simply, a company mission statement tells the world exactly why you're in business. As your company grows, such statements of purpose circulate throughout the organization so that your employees can develop strategies that support your overall mission and vision.

For Greg F., the fastener distributor in Downers Grove, Illinois, creating a mission statement was a matter of combining two business elements: selling fasteners and using the Internet for commerce. He says the result was a "general concept of the Internet and fasteners," joined together to produce a positioning statement for his firm—to sell the best-quality fasteners and to use the Internet as a primary means of commerce to do it.

"Our goal was to build the first and best fastener Web site," says Greg. "Then, over time, as things shook out with how the Internet was being used—and at what rate the fastener

Smart Tip

Because business incorporation offers the best form of protection for the wholesale distributor, it is the ideal structure for new entrepreneurs in this field. However, the wholesale distributor who—in the interest of time and money—chooses to get established as a sole proprietorship first can certainly incorporate in the future, once his or her company is up and running.

industry was going to adopt it—we were able to develop a more defined mission and figure out what we should be concentrating on."

Dierolf of Innovative Distribution Solutions says everyone is in business for two reasons: to create opportunities and to serve the needs of the customer. "Every mission statement needs to revolve around these two things. And [creating opportunities] should be number one, and customers should be number two," says Dierolf. "You have to serve the customer, but if for some reason you neglect the first part of the mission, then you'll end up a very unhappy business owner."

Perhaps the easiest way for a new distributorship to define its purpose is to drill down to its core business: buying from manufacturers and other sources, and selling to a defined customer base. From there, get introspective and decide what you'd like your company to be known for and how you can best convey these goals in a simple statement.

Business Structure

There are several choices of business structure for the wholesale distributor, though most business owners choose to incorporate through either an S corporation or LLC (limited liability company) status. Dierolf, who has much experience consulting with new, small wholesale distribution firms, says self-protection is the main reason to incorporate, but he recommends sole proprietorship to start-ups that can later switch to an incorporated structure.

According to Adam Fein of Philadelphia-based Pembroke Consulting Inc., many wholesale distributors with loyal, stable customer bases eventually end up being passed on from one generation to the next. "Many distributors today are second-, third-, and even fourth-generation entrepreneurs," he says. "And many wholesale distributors are mom-and-pop operations that tend to have many family members on the payroll."

When considering legal structures, it is wise for the new distributor to consider the fact that his or her business may last for multiple decades; this makes planning very important. A partnership formed with a nonfamily member that dissolves upon one partner's death may leave heirs an estate, but may leave the entrepreneur who wanted to carry on the business out in the cold.

Marshall M.'s wholesale distributorship of security hardware and locksmith supplies in San Diego is incorporated, but he recommends that new distributors try the LLC structure, namely because it gives distributors a "corporate defense." In other words, if something happens in your warehouse, or if someone decides to sue your firm for some reason, the business owner probably won't be liable personally as an "individual shareholder" in the company.

The Right Amount of Insurance

Wholesale distributors generally must carry the same amount and types of insurance that the typical company needs. This includes property and contents insurance, fire insurance, business interruption insurance, and other necessities that your insurance agent can discuss with you.

Don M., an Alexandria, Virginia-based wholesale wine distributor, says his firm is always "looking for and inquiring about insurance." He adds that in addition to normal business coverage, a few of his larger retail customers such as Sam's Club and Wal-Mart require an additional $2 million worth of business insurance. "This covers those retailers up to a certain dollar amount just in case one of our delivery people is on their property and has an accident," he says.

John M., a wholesale distributor of plumbing, heating, air conditioning, electrical, and other supplies in Lexington, Kentucky, advises new wholesale distributors to thoroughly review their policies with the appropriate insurance professional. "Your

Help! I Need Somebody!

When Keith S. started his Wickliffe, Ohio, wholesale distribution business selling men's belts and ties, he knew he wanted to incorporate it right away. Unfortunately, his financial situation didn't allow for the hiring of a lawyer to do the incorporation and an accountant to keep his books. The solution? He enlisted his accountant father to help him out.

"Those first few years were a real struggle," says Keith. "I credit my success to my father, who is an accountant and who handled my company's accounting and taxes those first couple years."

Because of his father's help, Keith estimates he saved about $5,000 annually. "That extra money, paid to someone to do tax returns, would have put me out of business during my first few years," he says, adding that Ohio, as well as various other states, distributes a helpful small-business packet that he utilized during his start-up. "As soon as you incorporate your company, there are so many tax issues that it can be a real nightmare if you don't know what you're doing."

suppliers will require you to have a good insurance policy in place in order to be satisfied that you are not likely to be burned out of business, and then not be able to pay your bills," he adds.

Obtaining the Right Licenses

Much like the insurance issue, licenses for new wholesale distributors are a fairly straightforward matter. You'll need an occupational license, as well as a license to collect sales and use tax if applicable. (For more information on sales tax, see Chapter 11 of this book.) Licensure requirements vary by state, so check with your state and local governments to obtain all the information you'll need to get started.

In addition to business licenses, distributors may consider becoming ISO 9000-certified. This designation is the standard for quality documentation in business. Put simply, it's a quality standard that can be used by corporations throughout the global

> **Bright Idea**
> Once your wholesale distribution business is up and running, you may wish to become ISO 9000–certified. Learn more about the process and what it's all about on the Web at "ISO Translated Into Plain English" (www.connect.ab.ca/~praxiom). Also, check out the ISO 9000 Directory at www.ISO9000directory.com, which contains various links and other information related to ISO 9000 certification.

community as a trademark for verifying the quality of services and product provided by a given distribution company. For example, a manufacturer in Korea who is ISO 9000-certified is working on the same quality standards as your ISO 9000-certified wholesale distribution firm in Boise, Idaho. So what's the importance of this certification for distributors? Basically, peace of mind and a knowledge that the products you're selling to customers will uphold your own standards, and that they won't disappoint your customers.

Professionals at Your Service

No man is an island—and neither is the aspiring entrepreneur. We all need help at one time or another, and professionals such as lawyers, accountants, and insurance agents can serve a valuable purpose throughout the life of your company. Other professionals such as marketing gurus and business consultants can also come in handy. For example, if your wholesale distribution business is going to have a store area, you'll want to enlist the knowledge of someone who has experience in merchandising.

Such professionals come at a price, of course, so shop around. For instance, if you need an accountant or financial consultant to help you determine the best way to incorporate your company, then be sure to do your homework ahead of time. Know what paperwork and numbers need to be in order before approaching a professional

Dollar Stretcher

Before choosing a professional from the Yellow Pages, take a look at your own circle of friends and family. Is there a lawyer who can help you incorporate? Or perhaps an accountant who will show you the ropes of corporate income taxes? Tapping into their knowledge banks can be beneficial during your business's early stages.

for help. Other professionals that may come in handy for a wholesale distributor on an independent consulting basis are experienced salespeople and purchasing professionals. If you can find one who is retired, or who will work for you on a short-term basis, you'll be able to learn a lot about sourcing, negotiating, selling, and pricing from such professionals.

Ask other professionals in your community to recommend the names of good business attorneys or accountants.

Once you've decided on your business name and structure, and after investigating your city and state laws regarding business licenses, you'll be ready to start thinking about how you're going to finance your new entity. In the next chapter, we will take a look at financing your wholesale distribution business, including how much money you'll need at start-up, how long it will take to get profitable, and what methods other distributors have used to get started.

5

Raising
Money

Ask any wholesale distributor what his or her biggest challenge was during the start-up phase and the answer is likely to be "raising money." It's a common gripe for small-business owners, who often have to get super creative when trying to get start-up capital, but one that can be overcome by determined entrepreneurs who believe in their dreams.

Pinpointing a Start-Up Number

While some industries seem to be able to raise money with a snap of their fingers, most have to take a more detailed approach to the process. Perhaps the best starting point is to figure out just how much you need.

In the wholesale distribution sector, start-up numbers vary widely, depending on what type of company you're starting, how much inventory will be necessary, and what

---

The Distributor's Start-Up Shopping List

Everyone loves shopping lists, so here's one that you can use as a guideline for getting your distributorship up and running. You'll need:

In the office

❑ Computer and printer

❑ Fax machine (or a multifunction machine that serves as printer/fax/copier and more)

❑ Telephones with multiple phone lines and some form of voice mail or answering machine

❑ Online access via dial-up or a high-speed line

❑ Office supplies (paper, pens, pencils, clipboards, etc.)

In the warehouse

❑ Pallet or racking systems to hold the product

❑ Forklift for moving goods

❑ A dock that delivery vehicles can back up to for loading and unloading goods

❑ Your start-up inventory (Read more about stocking up in Chapter 8 of this book.)

On the road

❑ Truck, van, or other method of delivery (For distributors shipping out of their delivery area, this means setting up an account with a nationwide delivery firm such as UPS or Federal Express.)

❑ Lift-gate accessibility (Even though you have a dock, your customers may not, so it's best to take your own lift-gate truck to their locations when making deliveries.)

---

type of delivery systems you'll be using. For example, Keith S., the entrepreneur who sells belts and ties from his basement in Wickliffe, Ohio, started his firm with $700, while Don M., the wine distributor in Alexandria, Virginia, required $1.5 million. While Keith worked from a desk and only needed a small area in which to store his goods, Don required a large amount of specialized storage space for his wines—and a safe method of transporting the bottles to his retailers.

The basic equipment needed for your new wholesale distributorship will be highly dependent on what you choose to sell. If you plan to stock heavy items, then you should invest in a forklift (some run on fuel or propane, others are man-powered) to save yourself some strain. Pallets are useful for stocking and pallet racking is used to store the pallets and keep them in order for inventory purposes.

According to Dave Spreen, branch manager for Tom Duffy Co., a flooring distributor in Eureka, California, a warehouse of sufficient size (based on the size of products you're selling and the amount of inventory you'll be stocking) is an absolute necessity. (Read more about leasing warehouse space in Chapter 6 of this book.) "You'll need to be able to move around efficiently, and that will require some type of racks to put pallets on," adds Spreen. "And be sure to leave room for twice the size of the forklift to be able to maneuver between racks of pallets and shelves in your warehouse."

According to Mark Dierolf of Innovative Distribution Solutions, some industry experts claim that "you can't start a distribution business with less than $1 million in capital." He disagrees but acknowledges that those who share the "$1 million" school of thought are probably thinking of businesses that require high inventory levels. "To be a true wholesaler, you must carry some inventory, but thanks to the way the flow of materials is going these days, inventory is getting to be a lot easier to obtain, depending on how you plan to sell your products," Dierolf explains. In other words, a tool distributor can have items shipped directly from the manufacturer to the customer without the customer realizing that the distributor didn't stock the item.

Dollar Stretcher

If bank financing proves elusive during your company's start-up phase, try tapping into your circle of friends, family, and business associates for help. Make them into official "investors" in your firm, and you'll be on your way to success!

"I don't think you need to have that much money to start a wholesale distribution company," says Dierolf. "In fact, you could feasibly start such a company with about $15,000 to $150,000, depending on what field you were getting into and the size of the market you wanted to cover." Dierolf adds that the determining factor—the thing that can really drive up that start-up cost number—is the type and amount of inventory that you plan to stock.

Getting Profitable

When it comes to securing financing, there's more to figuring out a number than just adding up the amount of equipment you'll need to get started. You'll also need to figure out how long it's going to take you to recoup the money you're investing or borrowing, and how long it will be before you're in the black.

At Don M.'s wholesale wine distributorship, figuring out how much inventory he needed to meet his financial goals was easy. The entrepreneur used (and continues to use) a simple formula, as follows:

Average wholesale price of a case of wine	$80
Hypothetical sales goal	$100,000
Inventory needed (divide the goal by the price of wine)	1,250 cases

The 1,250 number dictates the amount of inventory that the distributor will have to sell to reach that sales goal. With Don's gross profit margin (the amount of money left over after the product has been paid for) at 35 percent (at the high end for wholesale distribution) the formula reveals an average profit of $28 a case, or $35,000 annually, based on the example above.

Don adds that wholesale distributors who are able to spend a lot of time on their businesses—rather than outsourcing tasks to other companies—can reach those profit margins without much effort. "We have no middleman between ourselves and the manufacturer, and no brokers—both of which can raise your wholesale prices from the manufacturers."

Don't forget that wholesale distributors bring a lot more to the table than just facilitating the transfer of product from manufacturer to end user. For more information on value-added services in the distribution field, refer back to Chapter 2 of this book.

Looking for Financing

OK. You have rough estimates of how much money you need and how much you can make as a wholesale distributor. Now it's time to secure some financing.

For starters, you'll need to take a look at your own financial situation and determine how to tap into it without going broke in the process. It's a well-known fact that some entrepreneurs start their businesses on their personal credit cards (though we certainly don't advise this, it's worked for some) and with their savings.

If you're fortunate enough to have $50,000 or so to sink into your own wholesale distribution business, then go for it. However, be sure that you consult with any other account holders or family members before doing so.

Keith S. is one distributor who enjoys outsourcing work to other companies instead of keeping it in-house. Unfortunately, the banks don't seem to share his enthusiasm. When making loans, he says, many financial institutions take into consideration assets (machinery, equipment, real estate, etc.) and liabilities such as employees. For the entrepreneur working from the basement of his home and outsourcing functions like delivery, relabeling of products, and other duties, proving that you have assets is tough at best. Keith simply points the banks to his bottom line. He explains: "I tell them, look—do you care that I have a lot of machinery and equipment and that my profits are $50,000 a year, or would you prefer to see me outsourcing those functions and making $500,000 a year? I've found that from the bank's perspective, they actually are happier with the machinery."

> **Beware!**
> Before bringing any investors or partners into the fold of your new business, be sure to go over the legal ramifications of such an alliance with at least one attorney. Don't sign any contracts or accept any financing until you're sure the outside investment is going to be positive for your company's future.

> **Bright Idea**
> In search of bank financing? Check out your small, community banks first. These financial institutions have been bragging about their ability to truly service the small-business customer—the one who is often overlooked by larger banks that are chasing the big-dollar clients.

To solve the problem of raising money, Dierolf says the majority of new wholesale distributors rely on self-financing during the start-up phase. "Most of the folks who started their own distribution companies used $20,000, $100,000, or whatever other amount of their own money to get started," he says. "I also know several wholesale distributors who started their companies on five personal credit cards, though I wouldn't advise doing that."

Regardless of whom you plan to approach for financing assistance—a bank, family member, or business associate—develop a business plan for your new company first. This plan, which includes a competitive analysis, information on market strategies, and financial facts, serves as the backbone for any new company seeking start-up funds.

In the next chapter, we'll start hunting down a home for your new company. Whether you're going to start in your spare bedroom or in a 40,000-square-foot warehouse, you'll find out how to pick the right community, site, and facility for your new distribution firm.

Finding a
Home for Your
Company

When it comes to distribution, the old adage "location, location, location" holds true in some cases but certainly doesn't apply across the board. And while it is quite possible to start a small wholesale distribution business from just about anywhere, entrepreneurs who want to grow and prosper must at least be situated near transportation centers,

▲

Dollar Stretcher

If you can't afford warehouse space, try placing an ad in your local newspaper in search of "shared space." There are companies out there that just aren't making full use of their warehouses, and some may be willing to lease you a portion of space where you can store your goods.

especially if they plan to utilize shipping methods other than local delivery. Several other factors also come into play, so you'll want to read on to learn exactly what steps you'll need to take to secure the right location for your company.

Prime Locations for Wholesale Distributorships

Wholesale distributorships usually do not require high-traffic or high-visibility locations, but those that aren't homebased would be wise to find commercial space somewhere in the industrial section of town. Distributors should seek out areas that are rich in industry and close to transportation centers—especially if they are going to be shipping outside a 50-mile radius of their locations (this is the "normal" delivery area for most distributors, though the radius varies by company).

According to Pembroke Consulting's Adam Fein, desirable locations also vary by the type of product being distributed. "If you're an industrial distributor, for example, you'll want to be set up where the U.S. industrial base is, typically in the Midwestern states like Ohio, Michigan, Missouri, etc.," he advises. "Generally, however, wholesale distribution companies tend to locate where land is not too expensive and where they can buy or rent affordable warehouse space for the storage of inventory."

Fein adds that, for the most part, wholesale distributors are not located in downtown shopping areas. Instead, most are found "off the beaten path." If, for example, your company is a construction supply distributor that serves building or electrical contractors, your location will need to be accessible to those customers as they go about their daily routines.

The Right Site

Naturally, not every distributor needs a 40,000-square-foot warehouse situated in a major industrial park. In fact, Mark Dierolf of Innovative Distribution Solutions says location is really not a critical issue for the average small wholesale distributorship. However, any distributor who plans to sell "over the counter" to their customers—or have a walk-in showroom of some sort—would be wise to put some thought into his or her location. "For the most part, the critical issue for wholesale distributors is having good access to transportation," says Dierolf.

It can take time to find the perfect location for your business, so get an early start and don't give up.

John M., the Lexington, Kentucky-based wholesale distributor of industrial supplies, concurs and adds that location is highly dependent on the amount of exposure a distributor needs. He suggests picking a location that is "customer friendly" but doesn't require a lot of overhead expense. "We have showrooms for our products, so we think location is terribly important," he says. "We're located in a rural area, so we also need to be situated in a visible area, so our customers can find us." Because John's company includes five different wholesale distributorships, he often finds the need to expand and grow, which means even more locations. "When we open a new location or buy out an existing company, we always put a lot of thought into the physical plant," he says.

> ### Bright Idea
> As you search for your company's starter home, don't overlook your garage. Many wholesale distributors have moved their cars out into the driveway and made ample room for their new companies right in their garages. Set up a desk and computer in the corner and you have the perfect makeshift warehouse—all with a super-low overhead cost!

Home Court Advantage

Wholesale distribution is a versatile business. Because most of the time you'll be delivering products to your customers, as opposed to having them come to you, (though some distributors do have walk-up counters and storefronts), the average customer won't really know or care about where it's stored. For this reason, using your basement, garage, or spare bedroom as a starting point in business can make perfect sense.

> ### Smart Tip
> Look for warehouse space that's "material-handling friendly." In other words, you want a location where shipping and delivery will be easy, since that is a prime function of your business. Look for features such as shipping docks, multiple bays (so several trucks can be loaded and unloaded at once, if necessary), and lots of space.

"There are plenty of garage distribution companies that are making good profits," says Dierolf. "However, I don't think someone in the hills of Breckinridge, Colorado, could open a successful wholesale distribution business because there wouldn't be much of a customer base to serve. Being located two hours away from your nearest transportation hub in Denver, it would also be tough to ship and receive goods on a daily basis." That isolated situation notwithstanding, Dierolf says that the

Let's Make a Deal

Because your building lease is the biggest long-term commitment you'll have to make when starting your business, Alexandria, Virginia, wine distributor Don M. says to check out multiple sites and get prices on all of them. Then, pick the one you want and try to leverage your offers against one another. For example: If building A is the best candidate but more expensive than building B by $1 a square foot, try offering building A's owner $.50 less a square foot and justify it by telling him of your interest in building B and its lower price. Of course, this negotiating tactic isn't win-win for the landlord, so its success will depend heavily on the demand for commercial warehouse space in your area.

According to John M., the industrial supplies distributor in Lexington, Kentucky, another consideration when looking at prospective locations is leasehold improvements. In other words, anyone who wants to lease a building and then build it out to meet their requirements (e.g., add pallet racking, additional docking bays, etc.) should lease for a minimum of five years to really make use of those improvements.

John adds that the distributor should also retain the right to sublease the building in case his or her company grows out of the building during the lease term. That way, the distributorship won't lose money if it moves out early.

wholesale distributor who is located within 30 to 60 minutes of a transportation hub can certainly find success in a homebased setup.

Lease, Rent, or Buy?

If you decide to set up your company in a commercial location, you'll have three choices: lease space, rent space, or buy the building. For the most part, your decision will be between leasing and buying because, quite frankly, the owners will want you to occupy the space for at least a few years (renting is more of a short-term option). This can pose a problem for you in the very early stages, namely because you are never quite sure how quickly your business will—or, in some cases, will not—grow. While purchase prices for commercial locations vary greatly, Dierolf says lease rates for warehouses (which also vary by geographical location) range from $2.50 to $6 a square foot.

Don M., the Alexandria, Virginia-based wine distributor, recommends that all new wholesale distributors lease space whenever possible. He explains why: "One of the wonderful things about wholesaling, versus other manufacturing and retailing businesses, is that wholesaling locations are much less expensive. After all, you just need a flat-floor warehouse. It's not like a meat-processing plant, for example, where they have to have equipment like pulleys installed in the ceiling in order to operate properly."

John M. feels differently. He says that if the capital is there, go ahead and buy the facilities. "When we pick our locations, we try to pick them for their future value," he explains. "For instance if we want to be near a planned shopping center, or close to a place where two highways meet, we realize that those areas can become much more valuable and that the rents might eventually go up. However, if you own the building from the outset, then you don't have to worry about it, and it becomes an asset for your business."

Smart Tip

Homebased entrepreneurs in search of a location where they can negotiate with customers in person would be wise to check out the various office suites and meeting rooms in their areas. There, you can plop down a fee and meet with customers in a professional setting, away from your home office or warehouse.

Another advocate of leasing is Marshall M., the San Diego wholesale distributor of security hardware and locksmith supplies. He feels it's best for distributors to lease commercial facilities and to negotiate the shortest possible lease. Unfortunately, that's usually five years—but sometimes three if you can find the right landlord, according to Marshall. "That five-year commitment is probably the biggest commitment you'll have to make when your business is starting up," he says.

These days, location is becoming less and less of an issue for the entrepreneur looking to open his or her own business. As the Internet breaks down barriers between large and small companies, and as professional voice-mail services, marketing materials, and other tools formerly for highly capitalized firms become widely available, it's easier than ever to start a business from a spare bedroom. The average wholesale distribution firm can be started up anywhere, as long as there are manufacturers to buy from and customers to sell to.

In the next chapter, we'll give you the lowdown on exactly what you're going to need for your company's new home, including office equipment, distribution-related equipment, and a method of delivery for your products.

Setting
Up Shop

Once you've found a home for your new company, it's time to start thinking about how you're going to build it out to meet your needs. Building out includes the addition of equipment and other necessities to your warehouse, home, or other location to facilitate the shipping, receiving, and storage of goods.

Photo ©PhotoDisc Inc.

The Bare Necessities

How you set up your wholesale distribution business's interior is highly dependent on what type of product you're selling, the kind of facility it's housed in, and the methods of shipping and receiving you're utilizing. For example, the homebased entrepreneur selling small hand tools from his garage would probably need the following:

- Shelving units or some other storage and organizational implements
- Room for office space (details on setting up your office will follow later in this chapter)
- A method of getting the goods in and out of the garage (a sturdy, wheeled hand truck will do the trick for small, boxed items)

On the other hand, the entrepreneur who leases warehouse space for the wholesale distribution of, say, automobile tires, would need the following:

- Pallet racking and an appropriate number of pallets on which to store the tires
- A forklift for moving the tires into their respective positions, then removing them when the time comes to ship them to customers
- Room for office space
- A loading dock to facilitate shipping and receiving

While it may appear that the business of tires is more capital-intensive than that of small hand tools, a supervisor in a Florida-based wholesale tire distribution center assures us that it's not. He explains: "We know of a few local distribution centers that

It Adds Up

Here are a few approximate price ranges to help you figure out how much money you'll need to get your company up and running. We've based the prices on a hypothetical 5,000-square-foot warehouse.

	Low End	High End
Pallet racking (10 rows or sections)	$2,000	$20,000
Pallets	$40 each	N/A
Forklift (new)	$30,000	$40,000
Forklift (used)	$5,000	$12,000
Pallet truck (a piece of equipment used instead of a forklift to move pallets)	$750	$1,200
Shelving (10 rows or sections)	$1,000	$10,000
Hand truck	$75	$125
Office equipment setup (including basic PC, fax machine, telephone, etc.)	$2,500	$4,000
Office furniture (desk, chair, filing cabinets)	$500	$1,500

have the tires literally stacked on the floor. However, they do a lot less volume than we do, so it's a system that works well for them." (For more information on what it will take to get your wholesale distribution business up and running, refer back to "The Distributor's Start-Up Shopping List" on page 36.)

Standard Office Equipment

In addition to the necessary specialized equipment, your company is also going to need some basic office equipment and a safe place to house it. This space needs to be out of the way of forklifts, roaming eyeballs, and other hazards. At home, this probably won't be much of an issue because you can keep your office in the house, and your products in either the garage or thebasement. However, if the warehouse you're leasing doesn't have a separate office in it, you'll probably want to build one for yourself. This will take up 60 to 80 square feet, partitioned off by four walls, in the corner of the warehouse and near electrical outlets and phone jacks.

In your office, you'll need a sturdy desk, ergonomically correct office chair, telephone, fax machine, and filing cabinets where you can store all those paper-based orders, check stubs, and other necessary pieces of information.

Multiple phone lines (one or two regular lines, one fax line, and one modem line) will make your operations run smoothly, with the latter being irrelevant if you're using a high-speed cable modem, available through your local cable company. Certain Internet service providers (ISPs) and phone companies also offer high-speed digital lines, so check with your provider. If you're serving a customer base that's located outside your local calling area, you may also want to use a toll-free number. Customers placing orders and asking customer-service related questions will appreciate the fact that you're saving them money on long-distance phone calls.

When Keith S., a wholesale tie and belt distributor in Wickliffe, Ohio, started his business, he was lucky enough to already own a phone, computer, and fax machine. He created what he refers to as "fancy letterhead" by having an artist draw the company's name for him and then copying it onto blank paper. He was in business soon after that.

"That was it," Keith S. says. "I had saved one year's worth of income, and that was the amount of start-up cash that I had to work with." Depending on how many resources you have, you may be able to find used office furniture rather than buy everything new.

Few companies these days operate without a computer, and yours shouldn't either. At minimum, you'll need a PC with an operating system (most businesses use a Windows-based system), regular office software (spreadsheets, word processor, etc.), specialized software (if desired), and the necessary peripherals: a modem, printer, and scanner.

There are myriad options when it comes to distribution software. (See the Appendix of this book for the names and contact information of software providers for the distribution industry.) Prices vary widely, but the basic functions that a distributor needs are accounting (including receivables, payables, and expense tracking) and inventory control.

Greg F., president of a Downers Grove, Illinois, wholesale distributorship of specialty fasteners and components, says he uses a standard Gateway PC system (average cost: $1,500 to $2,000). He runs 95 percent of his business on the Microsoft Access and Microsoft Excel programs. "Access is, for my purposes, an excellent database program," says Greg F. "Even for a novice, it includes easy-to-develop custom applications, and it is extremely powerful." In terms of distributor-specific software packages, he says there's a wide range of software packages available, some costing as little as $500. And, he adds, there's certainly no shortage of high-end distribution software vendors.

While a high-end system contains all of the bells and whistles that a full-fledged distributorship might require, start-up wholesalers can definitely get by with a basic system, according to Greg. He explains: "For my purposes, it was easier to invest the time in learning how to use Microsoft Access and developing my own system. While it doesn't have all the features of commercial software, I know it inside and out. And when I want to add or modify a feature, I can do it myself."

At John M.'s five Kentucky-based distributorships, the technology requirements are a bit different. His company has 74,000 SKUs or stock keeping units (one SKU is assigned to each item that is stocked and sold) that require a mainframe computer and proprietary software for proper management. "If I were entering business today, I wouldn't have a mainframe because I can't imagine an entrepreneur starting big enough to warrant one," he comments. "Everything would be done on personal computers."

> ### Bright Idea
> As a wholesale distributor, you'll probably be dealing with multiple vendors, all of whom will want to send you their literature and catalogs. To keep things organized, dedicate one filing cabinet to such materials, and use alphabetized hanging folders—organized by product name—for easy accessibility when a customer calls and asks if you carry a particular product.

Get Those Wheels Rolling

In addition to your investments in a great location and the equipment necessary for getting it running smoothly, you'll also need to consider how necessary delivery vehicles will be. From there, whether you lease or buy your wheels is up to you. Generally, a leased vehicle requires less of a down payment. However, at the end of the lease, you turn in a vehicle that you've paid for and maintained for five or so years in exchange for . . . well, nothing. There are tax advantages to leasing vehicles, however, in that businesses can basically write off all expenses related to the truck, van, or car. It may be best to sit down with your accountant to figure out which method is best for you.

At Don M.'s Alexandria, Virginia-based wholesale wine distributorship, he says he finds it "easier to just buy" his company vehicles. His company started out small, however, and took a different route than most beverage distributors when it came to selecting a delivery vehicle: Rather than buy a large truck, he chose to buy a minivan. He explains: "One day I saw one of my competitors' trucks with the back door open. The truck contained about 60 cases of wine, but it was 90 percent empty." Today, Don says he still uses the minivans for regional distribution—and his competitors have followed suit. "They're more maneuverable than trucks are, and most are more cost-effective in terms of fuel," he explains.

According to John M., whether a new company leases or buys its vehicles is highly dependent on the amount of capital it has on hand. "Unless you have deep pockets, you will probably end up leasing vehicles," he says, adding that a start-up firm should start out with one delivery vehicle, then add on as the business volume grows. John owns all

Beware!
Leasing a company vehicle for five years may mean investing more and getting back less, especially if you've signed a separate maintenance agreement that inevitably forces you to buy the newer model to avoid high maintenance costs. To avoid this problem, give your lease contract a thorough examination and voice any concerns with the manufacturer before signing.

of his vehicles, namely because his industrial supply distribution business uses them "a lot longer" and runs them "a lot harder" than would be suitable for leased equipment.

In the end, whether you lease or buy depends on your individual needs, what type of financing you have and how long you plan to keep the vehicles or equipment in question. Be cautious when signing any long-term contracts, and realize that the equipment may become obsolete (especially computers, which are being upgraded at the speed of light) before the lease expires.

In the next chapter, we'll look at what type of inventory you'll need to get your business underway, where to find the merchandise to stock your shelves and how to get it into your customers' hands.

Inventory
Matters

In today's competitive business arena, companies are on perpetual diets. Owners and managers strive to run the leanest possible companies with the fewest employees and least amount of inventory and liabilities. In the distribution sector, some companies are being run with very low inventories—thus reducing their major sale (nonequipment) investments. Others

▲

Stock Tips

In San Diego distributor Marshall M.'s eyes, the distribution process is comparable to a platonic ideal. It's something you always strive for, he says, but that you can never get just right. The ideal, he says, is to maximize your fill rate (the rate at which you fill customer orders) while minimizing the amount of inventory on your shelves. "If a wholesale distributor had an infinite amount of dollars invested in inventory, then they would have an awesome fill rate," says Marshall, the security hardware and locksmith distributor. "However, that's a far-fetched ideal. Instead, it is best to minimize your investment so that you can be flexible, try new things, and work your way into new markets."

Unfortunately, Marshall says, distributors still struggle to fill customer orders quickly without having to sink every cent back into their inventories. Some try to solve it by getting "really economical," he says, and by thinning out their inventories. Then the customers start to squawk about poor fill rates. "It then turns into a slow-moving process, and customers will speak out loudly on fill rate issues because they've got to have their products quickly," he explains. "Then the pressure trickles down to your sales force, which is out on the front lines listening to the complaints."

In his years as a wholesale distributor, Marshall says he's still striving for that platonic ideal. He offers this piece of advice to start-up distributors: "The distribution game is all about who gets the biggest piece of the market. For that reason, I recommend all distributors go for a market where there are a lot of manufacturers in need of distributors who can get their goods into end users' hands."

choose to stock up in order to have "just what the customer ordered" on hand when the need arises.

There are caveats to both strategies. For starters, when a company chooses not to stock up, it runs the risk of being out of an item when the customer comes calling. At the same time, the distributors who overstock can find themselves in a real pickle if they can't get rid of merchandise they thought they could unload easily.

Being a distributor is all about "turning" inventory (selling everything you have in stock and then replenishing it)—the more times you can turn your inventory in a year, the more money you will make. Get the most turns by avoiding stocking items that may end up sitting in your warehouse for more than 90 days.

Luckily, there is a happy medium. Read on to find out how to balance the scales just enough to keep your company profitable and your customers happy.

Stocking Up ... or Not?

How much inventory you buy at start-up is going to depend heavily on exactly what you're selling, how far away your customers are located, and how demanding they are. For example, if you're supplying customers within a 20-mile radius of your warehouse with janitorial goods such as paper towels, rubber gloves, and hand soap, then you can base your stocking quantities on the number of customers multiplied by an average usage by each. Their usage is most easily determined by asking them just how much they normally procure on a monthly basis.

Smart Tip

Before investing in any inventory, do some thorough research on the marketplace. Instead of operating in a vacuum and assuming that you'll be able to unload whatever you can put your hands on, get some advice from manufacturers, customers, and even competitors in the industry. You may be surprised by what you find out!

On the other hand, if you are servicing a varied customer base located in different geographic areas, you may need to stock a little more than the entrepreneur in the previous example. Because you probably won't be visiting those customers at their locations, it may take a few months before you can determine just how much product they will be buying from you on a regular basis. Of course, you must also leave some breathing room for the "occasional" customer—the one who buys from you once a year and who will probably always catch you off guard. The good news is that having relationships with vendors can help fill those occasional needs quickly, even overnight or on the same day, if necessary.

According to Greg F. of the Downers Grove, Illinois-based fastener distributorship, stocking up is one of the tougher issues wholesale distributors have to deal with. Stock too much, he says, and you end up with a bunch of useless inventory (which, he adds, is the biggest expense a distributor has). Stock too little and your customers will go elsewhere when they find out how long it takes to get their hands on a particular item. The answer, he says, is to use your customers as a guide. "Don't try to use an across-the-board solution," he says. "Instead, try to keep as little inventory as possible and concentrate on the items that are most in demand."

At Keith S.'s wholesale belt and tie distributorship in Wickliffe, Ohio, all it took was a $700 investment in closeout ties to get started. He resold them to a drugstore, pocketed the profits, and reinvested the money in more inventory. It's a simple formula and one that works well for the small start-up entrepreneur who is operating with low overhead.

According to Kristi Tolman, vice president of corporate marketing for Tempe, Arizona-based Pinacor Inc., a distributor of technology products, for a distributor who has already invested in a location, vehicles, and other necessities, inventory needs really depend on the product life cycle. The one with the longer life cycle (hand tools, for example) is less risky to stock, while the one with the shorter life cycle (food, for example, usually has a short life cycle) can become a liability if there are too many of them on the shelf. "The shorter the life cycle, the less product you're going to want to have on hand," says Tolman.

Pinacor's Tolman says that ultimately, the wholesale distributor's goal is to sell the product before having to pay for it. In other words, if you are buying computers, and if the manufacturer offers you 30-day payment terms, then you'll want to have less than 30 days' worth of inventory on the shelf. "In the distribution business, you don't ever want to end up 'owning' inventory," she advises. "If you still haven't sold it by the time you have to pay for it, then the whole profit model falls apart on you."

The following list sums up the tricks to stocking a wholesale distributorship:

- Don't overdo it when it comes to buying inventory.
- Try to get a grasp on your customers' needs before you invest in inventory.
- If you can get away with doing it cheaply at first (especially those with low overhead), then go for it.
- Be wary of investing too much in products with short life cycles, which you may get stuck with if they don't sell right away.
- Stock up to a level where you can sell the product before you have to pay for it.

Going Straight to the Source

No wholesale distributorship would be able to function without good sources of product, which are usually either manufacturers or other distributors. The number of vendors you deal with depends on how varied your own offerings are, how efficient (timely deliveries, good prices, nice to deal with, etc.) the individual vendors are, and how picky your customers are about brand (for example, you may need to deal with a specific manufacturer or distributor if you have a large-volume customer who will only buy a particular brand of hard hats for a construction site).

Greg F. in Downers Grove, Illinois, says he uses "very few" sources for the parts he sells. "Though my vendor database has more than 150 companies in it, I buy 90 percent of my parts from less than 10 of those companies," he comments. However, before getting started as a wholesale distributor, Greg says it is "extremely important to have some type of relationship established with as many vendors as possible."

Bright Idea

Trade shows are a great place to meet up with manufacturers and other suppliers in a setting where you can view their products and catalogs and talk to their sales reps. Flip through your industry's trade magazine, or contact an industry trade group for information on upcoming shows.

Howdy, Partner!

For years, companies have made decisions concerning where to buy parts, supplies and services based solely on price. Times have changed. Today, these very companies are turning their attention to what consultants refer to as "relationship marketing," to meet the challenges of boosting profits, increasing market share, and enhancing competitive position in an increasingly global and cost-conscious marketplace.

The process, which calls for building long-term connections to suppliers and customers, is making companies rethink their whole approach to purchasing and selling. Effective partnering is accomplished through well-established, long-term relationships; a concentration on win-win relationships that benefit both parties; and by working together as true business partners, instead of simply acting like vendors and customers.

Here's the trick for wholesale distributors: Rather than focusing on price alone, scrutinize more closely from whom you're buying, what you're buying, how you buy and what you're paying. By partnering with key vendors to reduce costs, wholesale distributors have managed to save money on their bills for purchased goods. In addition, many distributors, who are essentially acting as suppliers to their own customers, are using the same tactics and forming similar relationships with their valued customer base.

Keith S. cautions new distributors against becoming too reliant on just a few suppliers and says that at the outset, his own firm became reliant on one supplier and one customer for 80 percent of its business. "Five months after I left my full-time job, the supplier stopped supplying me the products," he says. "I was dead in the water." To solve the problem, Keith changed the focus of his company from one that bought salesmen's samples to one that bought product directly from manufacturers. "I relied on my ability to sell consumer products and started to sell for small manufacturers that needed help in my geographic territory," he says. "Eventually, I increased my cash flow and got back on my feet."

Like Keith, most wholesale distributors spend their time trying to perfect the balance between vendor and customer. To find good vendors, distributors should visit industry trade shows, read trade magazines (both articles and advertisements), and approach manufacturers directly. Often, the best chance to represent a product line

Beware!
Before signing any exclusive partnering contracts with vendors or customers, consult with an attorney.

will come if your distributorship is in a region where a manufacturer has poor or no representation. Check out each carefully before taking on its lines, and remember that your own reputation will be affected by the product quality and the service provided by the supply sources you select.

Once you've found a few good sources of product, the next step will be to establish a working relationship with them. Translation: You need to establish credit with your sources. Because distributors usually have to wait 10 to 30 days to be paid by their own customers (typical invoice terms are net 30 days), they must negotiate similar or better terms with their suppliers to avoid paying out money they don't have. The solution is to establish credit with your suppliers.

"Because I had relationships with many of my initial vendors, it was not difficult to establish credit," comments Greg F. "And by always paying my core vendors well and using them as credit references, I have basically been able to establish credit whenever needed."

While Greg F. may have had it easier than most new wholesale distributors, John M. of the Lexington, Kentucky-based industrial supply distributorship says you can count on every supplier taking a "good hard look" at your financial statement and your ability to pay your bills. "The stronger you are financially, the better deal you are going to be able to make," he adds. "They'll take a look at your business, and the terms you can negotiate will directly reflect the soundness of your start-up company, including what kind of financial backing you have and what your viability is in the marketplace."

For example, if there are already two or three companies similar to yours in close proximity, then your company will look "a bit more risky" according to John. And it's not just because of the tight market—it's also because the manufacturer won't want to step on the toes of its existing customers. "They probably won't want to offend the two or three companies that are already doing business with them and paying their bills, just to take a long shot on a new company," he says.

To avoid potential conflict, thoroughly research your market prior to making any decisions about what products you're going to sell. (Read more about market research in Chapter 3 of this book.)

From Supplier to Customer

The next critical step in setting up your business is to establish a few relationships with freight carriers and shipping companies. Even if you're only delivering to your

Bright Idea

When deciding on shipping methods, don't overlook the fact that many manufacturers will "drop ship" (ship directly to customers on your behalf) product to customers for you, especially for rush shipments.

local area, you should always be prepared to handle things like incoming shipments that aren't handled properly by the manufacturer, local customers who may want a big shipment sent 1,000 miles away, and other situations that can crop up.

At Greg F.'s wholesale distributorship, freight costs average about 2 percent of his company's total sales. He says the majority of his products are shipped via UPS or Federal Express, though he does offer delivery to his local customers. "This service has been very helpful in keeping accounts that might otherwise shop [around for] parts," he says.

To set up relationships with carriers (including overnight companies such as Federal Express, ground shipping companies like UPS, and over-the-road trailers such as SAIA), it's simply a matter of calling their local office and setting up a business account. After a credit and reference check, the company will set up a merchant account for you, and will either stop by at a regular time each day or when you call them, depending on the frequency of shipments. Be sure to investigate liability coverage before a package gets lost. You might need additional insurance.

Now that we've covered many of the operational, equipment, and inventory issues involved in starting up a wholesale distribution firm, we'll move into new territory: human capital. In the next chapter, we'll give you details on how to attract and retain the right employees to help you run your new company.

9

Finding the Rest
of Your Team

If it were humanly possible, most entrepreneurs would stick to running one-person operations. Unfortunately, this would severely inhibit company growth and at the same time completely burn out the average business owner. For these reasons, it's wise to consider hiring employees as your company grows.

Photo ©PhotoDisc Inc.

If your wholesale distribution firm started out as a one-person operation, then your first new hire will probably be a jack-of-all-trades type of assistant who can mimic many of your own moves. As your firm grows, you can add more specialized positions such as warehouse manager, sales representatives, and office staff.

Staffing the Right Way

Once your wholesale distribution company gets up and running, you will want to hire employees as it becomes necessary. How will you know when it's necessary? Well, when your employees start wearing more than five hats, or when you realize that working 24 hours a day wouldn't even help you get caught up, you know it's time to hire help.

For starters, you'll want someone who can manage customer relations. This person would handle inbound and outbound telephone calls to customers, as well as letters, faxes, and e-mails to and from customers regarding issues, concerns, and questions. "These can be individuals who have recently graduated from college, or that have some sales experience," says Kristi Tolman of Tempe, Arizona-based Pinacor Inc., a distributor of technology products. "You should hire individuals who are aggressive and very sensitive to customer service needs."

Next up on the hiring list will be someone who can run your company's finance department. This employee's duties will include verifying customer credit, working with third-party organizations (leasing companies, for example), and handling other financial issues for the company. This person should have a financial background or credit management experience.

As you begin to delegate more responsibilities to your employees, you'll also need to determine who is going to handle the purchasing function. When the time comes to hire someone specifically for purchasing, that person will find himself or herself working directly with your vendors to negotiate prices and delivery time frames. He or she will also manage the inventory in your warehouse or distribution center. Another consideration, which may or may not be necessary, depending on where you're located and how much of your business is done by referral, will be a marketing professional. This person should be experienced in the field and will be responsible for presenting your company to your customer base, vendors, media, trade groups, and other entities in a positive fashion.

> **Tip...**
>
> **Smart Tip**
> Giving up control isn't easy, but your business can't grow if you don't hire employees. Take it slow, and hand-pick your new workers carefully. In the long run, you'll be glad you relinquished certain duties to others so you could concentrate on the tasks you enjoy!

Once your front office is staffed, you'll need to hire a few warehouse associates who will physically take inventory off of the shelf, pack it in boxes, and receive incoming inventory. They will also operate the forklifts in the warehouse and handle other tasks as needed. Depending on how your company is set up, you'll probably need a warehouse manager as well. This person should have some warehouse experience and will spend most of his or her time worrying about control and efficiency and making sure workers are filling orders correctly. At Don M.'s wholesale wine distributorship in Alexandria, Virginia, for example, his warehouse manager ensures that the right wine is put into the right cases for the customer, that the trucks are loaded, and that the delivery people are on time in delivering it.

How Much You'll Have to Pay

Pay rates for employees in the distribution field vary greatly by geographic area. As with any other type of business, for example, a warehouse in midtown Chicago will probably pay more for workers than would a warehouse located in a rural Iowa town.

On average, an office manager or assistant will demand $10 to $18 an hour, depending on experience. According to Pinacor's Kristi Tolman, any of the professional positions (purchasing or marketing associates, for example) will command a yearly salary in the $30,000 range. "It does vary by geography, but you can pretty much assume that an entry-level associate will command a salary somewhere in the $30,000 range, with a slightly more experienced associate commanding more."

Tolman says that salaries paid to warehouse workers are very much dictated by the geographic location and what other businesses are nearby. According to Keith S. of the Wickliffe, Ohio-based wholesale accessories distributor, salaries for workers "vary greatly based on whether you're in an urban or metropolitan market." He pays workers $7 an hour and lets them choose their own hours. "We attract great, loyal workers because larger companies with bigger warehouses may pay $10 per hour for them, but we are extremely flexible," Keith adds.

On average, warehouse workers command anywhere from minimum wage to $7 an hour to start. Pay rates for office personnel range from $8 to $15 an hour, depending on experience, and warehouse managers generally earn $25,000 a year and up, depending on their experience in the field.

Alternatives to Traditional Employees

If the numbers listed above sound like a lot to shell out during the start-up phase, there are alternatives. These days, nontraditional work styles are common and tend to be flexible. For example, you can outsource your credit department to a firm that specializes in such functions. There are even "virtual assistants" that you can hire on a per-project basis via the Internet, and you don't even need to provide desk space for them!

For John M., owner of the Lexington, Kentucky, wholesale distributorships of industrial equipment and supplies, including air conditioners, it's usually the summertime that finds him scrambling for extra hands around the warehouse. When the need arises, he calls on temporary workers to help out. He uses temps in positions such as loading and unloading trucks, where product knowledge is unnecessary and training is minimal. "If a lot of technical know-how is required, then temps don't work well," says John, adding that temps come in very handy when employees take temporary leaves (such as medical or maternity leave). "They can be very helpful, particularly for a new, start-up business."

Don M. concurs: "The warehouse is one area where we've found contract associates to be very effective. As our business goes through cycles, we're able to fill in with temporary workers. We use them in positions that don't require a long learning curve—where we can quickly train them and get them up to speed."

Keith S.'s company relies heavily on outsourcing rather than full-time employees. He employs two people in a warehouse but

---

Dollar Stretcher

If you don't want to hire an in-house marketing professional, try outsourcing the work to an independent contractor. There are many homebased workers in this field who handle projects (creating marketing materials, designing logos, etc.) for a variety of clients. Try Guru.com (www.guru.com) or FreeAgent.com (www.freeagent.com) to find independent contractors online.

This Is How We Do It

One might assume that a wholesale wine distributorship would want to hire salespeople who know something about wine. Not a wine expert, of course, but at least someone who knows the difference between their zinfandels and their chardonnays.

Not at Don M.'s Alexandria, Virginia-based wholesale wine distributorship. In fact, he says he won't even interview a prospective salesperson who presents himself or herself as a "connoisseur of wine."

"We want salespeople who say 'Yeah, this is wine, but it might as well be ice cubes,'" says Don. "They need to be completely unattached from the product." In addition to the detachment, he also looks for drive in his salespeople, and sales experience in a variety of industries.

When it comes to hiring for other positions, Don says he looks for different traits. For administrative workers, for example, he's seeking "KSA," or knowledge, skill, and attitude. "They're the type of employee you want to stay in the office and worry about the numbers, the follow-up letters and the taxes," he says. "My job as an executive is to hire one type of person for sales and a completely different person to be, say, an office manager."

outsources everything else, including sales and marketing. "Until a company is making $2 to $3 million in annual sales—and able to afford an executive and administrative staff—I truly believe that everything should be outsourced," he says.

Beware!

Don't neglect to check the references on your prospective employee's resume before making a decision to hire them. It's easy to make a fancy-looking resume these days. Dig down past the fluff and make sure the job experience is as solid as it looks on paper.

Tips for Finding Employees

It's a problem companies of all sizes and across all industries experience at one time or another: You just can't keep good employees. In distribution, it's no different.

For the small entrepreneur to put months into training an employee only to have him or her leave for another job can be truly devastating. To prevent this from happening too often (OK, even we know you can't keep it from happening sometimes!), try following these tips for recruiting and retaining employees:

▲

- *Offer them enough money.* If a truck driver comes to you for a job and if he was already making $15 an hour, then you know that offering him $9 an hour won't work. Even if he does take the pay cut, he'll only leave when something better comes along. The solution? Stick to hiring employees who have been making the same or less than what you're willing to offer.

- *Explore their potential.* If you're looking for an administrative assistant who will remain your administrative assistant, then look for the appropriate credentials to fill that need. However, if you want an assistant who can be groomed into a salesperson and essentially "grow up" through your company, then look for the credentials that will meet the position's needs.

- *Search outside your area.* Try placing employment ads in newspapers outside your local area—preferably in an area with a higher unemployment rate, such

Dollar Stretcher

If you're looking for inexpensive labor, why not check out your local community college or university for an intern? They come cheap, and many could use the experience that a hands-on, entrepreneurial start-up will give them.

Let Them Eat Cake

These days, it's hard to predict just what will make your employees walk out the door for another job. For the small company that relies on employees who wear multiple hats, watching the door slam behind a valued employee can be a real blow. But sometimes it's hard to pinpoint what employees really want. Is it more money? More free time? Better health benefits?

According to a recent poll, it's food. That's right: Complimentary food and drinks ranked fifth on a list of more common perks offered to recruit retail workers by 129 firms recently polled by Ceridian Employer Services, a Minneapolis human resources consultancy.

Casual dress (which is quite common in a wholesale distribution setting anyway) and flexible hours (something you may wish to consider offering to employees who request it) ranked highest.

Farther down on the list were telecommuting, allowing pets at work, lactation rooms, and on-site child care.

as a city where a large plant may have recently shut down.

- *Cultivate, cultivate, cultivate.* Everyone wants to feel wanted, and that includes your employees. When you find a great warehouse workers or purchasing agents, be sure to foster their professional and personal growth by allowing them to share

ideas and truly be a part of your growing organization.

> **Bright Idea**
>
> If you're lucky enough to have a large, hard-working family (or extended family), then now is the time to tap into their strengths and put them to work for your new company.

As a wholesale distributor, the primary obstacle to finding and keeping good employees in a warehouse atmosphere is that you'll be competing with many other companies for the same skill sets. In other words, a warehouse worker would also make a good assembly line worker or auto detailer. The key is to choose carefully and to make your employees feel like they're part of a team and not just another laborer. The same goes for your sales staff and administrative personnel. Such jobs are adaptable across a variety of industries, so be sure to treat employees well, make them feel they're contributing to the overall success of the company, and listen to their needs.

Keeping Them Happy

It used to be that small, start-up firms could get away with not offering their employees health insurance. No longer. Everyone from the two-person operation to the 2,000-employee conglomerate offers health insurance these days. Once you start hiring employees, you'll need to offer some sort of health insurance.

But it doesn't have to kill your budget. There are various trade organizations (see the Appendix of this book) you can join to get group rates, and you can also negotiate with your employees on the percentage that each of you will pay. Most employees understand that a start-up probably won't foot the entire bill, but dividing the costs 50/50 or even 75/25 can make it more fair. Down the road—as your business becomes profitable—you can review the agreement and renegotiate if necessary. (You might want to put a time frame on that promise if the employees are reluctant to pay their portion. Tell them you will renegotiate it in one year, for example.)

"As a wholesale distributor, you want to offer health insurance to your employees," says John M. "It's practically mandatory in most marketplaces today. It can make a dramatic difference between someone wanting to work for you and not wanting to work for you." As the exception to the rule, John cites the example of the two-person family where both spouses are working. As long as one is working and has health insurance, then the issue is not such a sticking point in the hiring process. If only one is working and doesn't have health insurance, then the family is in bad shape. "The health insurance issue is much more important for wholesale distributors than it was, say, 20 years ago," he adds.

In the Appendix of this book you'll find a comprehensive listing of associations and professional organizations for the distribution industry. If purchasing health insurance on your own is out of the question financially, then it would be wise to contact a few of these groups to see what type of rates they can offer members. Whatever method you choose, the important thing is to keep your hard-earned employees happy, safe, and productive.

In the next chapter, we'll show you how to get word of your new company out to the rest of the world. We'll also give you an inside look at how wholesale distributors are using the Internet to expand their businesses and how they keep their customers coming back for more.

Getting
the Word Out

Now that you have the scoop on how to staff your company and keep your employees happy and healthy, it's time to get those customers beating down your door. The majority of wholesale distribution firms work both in a direct-selling fashion (calling, faxing, or e-mailing customers to sell their wares) and by word-of-mouth (the referral system).

However, you can get a jump on your competitors by testing out some of the more advanced strategies we'll discuss in this chapter.

The Advertising Hook

When was the last time you saw an ad for a wholesale distribution company in your local newspaper? Probably never, and for good reason. Running a newspaper ad would mean shelling out too much money to reach too broad an audience. Instead, you'll have to get more creative and ferret out the magazines and trade journals your potential customers are reading. For example, if you're distributing cutting tools, then you'll want to advertise in places such as *Cutting Tool Engineering*, a magazine that caters to your audience.

One of the most effective ways for distributors to advertise is through highly targeted ads directed at specific consumer demographics. For example, a distributor of technology components whose customer base includes computer resellers would advertise in publications that are specifically targeted at that customer base. And by utilizing action-based ads (those that include a strong call to action—call by a certain date and save 10 percent on your first order, for example), distributors can get the phone ringing by creating a sense of urgency.

No Advertising Allowed? No Problem!

It's a commonly known fact that most wholesale distributors choose not to advertise. In fact, the majority would rather do their business by word-of-mouth referrals, direct contact with customers, and cold-calling new prospects.

However, some wholesalers would like to advertise but simply cannot. And it's not because of budgetary reasons—it's the law. Just ask Don M., owner of the wholesale wine distributorship in Alexandria, Virginia. In his state, advertising the sale of alcoholic beverages is illegal, so he relies solely on his outside sales team to get out and meet the customers in person.

And while one would think that this barrier would hurt the wine wholesaler, Don says quite the opposite is true. He explains: "It's actually kind of nice because we are a very small wholesale distributor, but we can be on par with our 100-year-old competitors who are making $40 to $50 million in sales annually. Nobody can advertise, so the playing field is completely leveled in that regard."

Beware!

Expect to be approached by various advertising representatives as soon as you open your doors. From your daily paper to your local weekly to the neighborhood alternative lifestyle newspaper, they'll all approach you to advertise in their publications. Check out each carefully, and be sure the publication is reaching your target audience before shelling out any money for advertising.

While there is no "typical" advertising budget for wholesalers, namely because some firms just don't advertise, most firms set their advertising budgets based on a percentage of forecasted annual sales. The amount varies wildly depending on the distributor's industry. Keith S. of the Wickliffe, Ohio, wholesale men's accessories distributorship says his firm doesn't advertise at all. Instead, he utilizes face-to-face selling and trade shows to get his customers interested in his products. At the San Diego-based distributor of security hardware and locksmith supplies, Marshall M. advertises monthly in trade publications for his industry. "Each industry has its own, and there are two primary magazines for ours," he says. "We also participate in all industry trade shows, events, and association meetings." According to Marshall, his firm's ad budget is based on revenues. In addition, the company has partnership programs—known as co-op advertising—in which the distributor shares advertising expenses with product manufacturers.

According to Mark Dierolf of Gilbertsville, Pennsylvania-based Innovative Distribution Solutions Inc., the wholesale distributor that is willing to shell out a bit of money for advertising is the one who will stand out from its competitors. Overall, he says, the wholesale distribution sector is a poorly marketed industry. "If somebody would just be willing to spend $2,000 to $5,000 annually on advertising—$5,000 being the preferred level—they would really see a difference," says Dierolf, adding that this amount is perfect for the distributor who is doing $250,000 to $1 million in annual sales. "This can include some custom signage, a few bulk mailers, and a small advertising program for a localized area."

The PR and Promotions Game

It's a bit more time-consuming, but it's definitely less expensive than placing ads in magazines. It's call PR or public relations, and it works. This strategy involves preparing press releases—announcing your new company, business milestones, or other newsy events—and sending them to your local radio, TV, and newspaper outlets, along with your industry's trade magazines. It's a strategy that requires much follow-up with editors, journalists, and publishers. However, just one media placement—at no charge—can pay for the efforts in one fell swoop.

Among the wholesale distributors we interviewed for this book, PR wasn't nearly as popular as promotions were. Most prefer to host special events and open houses to create goodwill, attract new customers, and make their existing customers feel special.

For example, Don M. says his company started the wine tasting trend in his home state of Virginia back in 1987. As a small wholesale wine distributor of primarily specialty, high-end wines, he says he realized early on that his company would have to do something special to stand out from the crowd of heavily advertised Gallo and Inglenook wines crowding the grocery shelves. "We offered the wine tasting to our retailers during the high-traffic times—Friday evenings and Saturdays," he explains. "It really caught on, and now our big competitors are [doing] the same thing."

And it's not just Don's competitors that took notice of the events' effectiveness. Recently, a new supermarket in Virginia contacted him about doing wine tastings in a new store with a wine section on the second floor, accessible by elevator. "This gave us the inroads to get our product lines on the shelves more easily than our competitors did because this store is not interested in the big-volume wines."

Beware!

Don't throw your money away for an advertisement in a magazine that might not reach your targeted audience. Investigate by asking for a media kit from the magazine. This will give you the CPM (or cost per thousand, or how much it costs you to reach 1,000 readers) of your advertisement, detailed information on the publication's readership, and other valuable information.

Hanging Out Your Shingle

Bright Idea

Here's an inexpensive way to promote your company: Compile a list of potential customers by using your local phone book, trade directories, the Internet, and other sources. Then create mailers or postcards (available at your local office supply store) announcing your new company and its offerings.

Because many start-up wholesale distribution companies work from warehouses in industrial parks; small, out-of-the-way locations; and even from home, signage is not usually an issue. For larger companies that have walk-up counters and storefronts, however, it's a different story. Such companies should have both a roadside sign (located at the front of the industrial park's entrance road, for instance) and a sizable sign on the building.

According to Marshall M., a good-sized sign with a company logo, placed on top of the warehouse or building, is very necessary for wholesale distributors. "It helps create branding and recognition," he says. Each of his company's locations includes a "will call" area that looks like a showroom. It includes samples of his firm's products, signage from various manufacturers, special offers, and promotional fliers. "It basically looks and feels like a store with merchandise," Marshall adds. "In these 'will call' areas, customers can come in and make purchases in person."

Jumping on the World Wide Web

These days it seems like every business has a Web presence—and with good reason. According to the Boston Consulting Group, one-fourth of all U.S. business-to-business purchasing is expected to be done online by 2003, reaching $2.8 trillion in transaction value. Because as a wholesale distributor you'll be dealing solely on a business-to-business basis, the Web is sure to become a major part of your company sometime in the future.

> ## Dollar Stretcher
>
> If you're going to outsource the construction of your company's Web site, be sure to shop around. Pricing on such services really runs the gamut, depending on what you need and who you ask. The first Web designer you come across might do great work, but the next might do acceptable work for a much lower price.

For Greg F. of the Downers Grove, Illinois-based wholesale fastener distributorship, the Web is a vital selling tool. He says the typical Web site—built from scratch by a Web designer and hosted by an outside source—would cost about $10,000, maybe less, depending on the features included. Of course, there are myriad firms online that will build a Web site at no charge and then take a cut of sales (Frontiernet.com at www.frontiernet.com, for example). "Most distributors view the Web as an advertising medium and not as a dynamic selling tool," says Greg. "The distributors who are really forward-thinking, and who will end up dominating, are the ones who aren't just looking for a Web page but who are asking 'How can I make my site perform? How can I make it better than everyone else's? How can I enable it for online commerce?'"

Greg adds that distributors would be wise to sit up and take notice of how the Web is affecting their line of work. "In my opinion, the Internet is going to tear down the existing fastener distribution world and rebuild it in a very different way," he says. "The Internet is going to eventually take all the mystery out of sourcing and, to some degree, put all distributors on an even level." He says that Yahoo! (www.yahoo.com) has been one of the most effective search engines for him, thanks to its organization.

▲

"With a few clicks, I can scroll through links to hundreds of potential sources and customers," he says.

It All Comes Down to Customer Service

We've given you the information you need to advertise and promote your new wholesale distribution business, but now we're going to share with you the real secret to winning customers. It can be summed up in three simple words: superior customer service. Without it, your business will not prosper. With it, your company will stand head and shoulders above the rest.

"Distribution customers rarely purchase from one distributor, so winning customers is a daily task," says Kristi Tolman of Tempe, Arizona, technology products distributor Pinacor. "The secret is to develop a very strong relationship with customers, understand their needs, and make sure they choose you for more than price and availability, namely because it's difficult to win in a game that is played by nothing more than those two factors." To ensure that the "game" is played on more than just price and availability, Tolman suggests going out and spending time at customer locations and hiring employees who truly understand the value of building customer relationships. "Distributors really have to be sensitive to building those relationships," she adds.

According to John M. of the Lexington, Kentucky, industrial supply distributorship, the best customer service strategy a distributor can use is a simple saying: "The customer is always first." It's a strategy that works across all industries. "One of the big secrets to success in this industry involves offering your customers something that the 'other guy' cannot," he suggests. For example, the typical hardware customer cannot get a one-on-one conversation going with a knowledgeable individual when they walk into a huge retail hardware store. But at John's small hardware distributorship, they can. "Those other stores are impersonal, and customers tend to get lost in the big stores," he adds. "The key to successful customer service is giving them an atmosphere where they feel comfortable doing business and where they can get their questions answered by someone who knows the right answers."

While customer service certainly plays a major role in the success of any distributorship, the way the company presents itself to the rest of the region, state, nation, or world is really what gets those customers in the door in the first place.

> ### Tip...
>
> ### Smart Tip
>
> If you are running your wholesale distribution business from a warehouse, be sure to mark the entrance to the office area clearly (above the door is fine) so that visitors who wander in can easily locate it.

Whether you choose to advertise your business or simply rely on word-of-mouth referrals to bring in that business depends on your situation. Whatever your decision, you now have the marketing tools that will help your company get noticed. In the next chapter, we'll show you how to manage your finances, including handling sales taxes and other pertinent issues that go along with owning your own wholesale distribution business.

Financial
Management

Now for the fun stuff. Not many entrepreneurs enjoy the number-crunching and bean-counting part of being a business owner, so we've broken down the steps for you in hopes of making the process a little less painful. Basically, your function as a distributor involves paying vendors and collecting payments from customers. The "spread" (or amount that's left over) is your gross profit. In this chapter, we'll show you how to manage that bottom line and handle the bookkeeping issues that most affect wholesale distributors.

For distributors, the biggest challenge is running your business on low operating profit margins. Adam Fein of Philadelphia-based Pembroke Consulting Inc. suggests getting your operations as efficient as possible and turning inventory around as quickly as possible. "These are the keys to making money as a wholesale distributor," he says.

And while the operating profit margins may be low for distributors, Fein says the projected growth of the industry is quite optimistic. Sales by wholesale distributors are expected to match or exceed the growth rate for the overall U.S. economy. Growth should be steady, and sales are expected reach $2.8 trillion by the early 2000s. According to the Department of Commerce, gross profit margins for wholesale distributors have been "remarkably steady" at about 21 percent of sales over the past decade. (Gross margins as a percent of sales are expected to remain at about the same level over the next few years.)

Playing the Markup Game

In its most basic form, wholesale distribution is all about the "spread" or profit margin between what you paid for the product and what you got when you sold it. The bigger the spread, the bigger the profits. For example, in the wine business, Alexandria, Virginia-based Don M. boasts a 30 percent profit margin. People place great value on high-end wines, so they're willing to pay more for bottles of chardonnay than they will for, say, computer modems.

But Don M.'s "spread" isn't typical for wholesale distributors. From Mark Dierolf's experiences consulting with new and existing wholesale industrial distributors, the average profit margin for wholesale distributors is between 2 and 4 percent. "If you can make 6 percent, then you are doing pretty well," says Dierolf, president of Innovative Distribution Solutions in Gilbertsville, Pennsylvania. "I'm not saying you can't get a 12 percent return, but the average is 2 to 4 percent."

According to Paul Lineback, vice president and general manager of Pyramid Products Inc., a Spokane, Washington, wholesale distributor of golf ball displays, most distributors use the following formula when it comes to markup: If it costs the manufacturer $5 to produce the product, and they have a 100 percent markup, then you (the distributor) buy it for $10. Following the same formula, the wholesaler would double the cost and sell it for $20. Thus, there is a 400 percent markup from manufactured price to the wholesaler's customer.

According to John M. of the Lexington, Kentucky-based industrial equipment and supply distributorships, where your company is located can play a major role in what kind of markup you can get on your products. In metropolitan areas, he says, distributors get less of a markup because they normally do a much higher volume than a rural distributor. However, because that rural distributor is often the "only game in town," bigger markups are possible. Says John, "Often, it is cheaper for someone to buy their products for 10 percent more than it is for them to drive 25 miles to go pick it up, or have it shipped."

Managing Your Cash Flow

When you step back and look at the way the money flows in the manufacturer-distributor-customer relationship, it's not hard to see that the person in the middle may end up dealing with some special issues when it comes to cash

Beware!
Don't assume that just because your company is located in a rural location that you can gouge customers with high prices. These are the days of the educated consumer. Remember that customers can now use the Internet to access product and pricing information with just a few clicks of the mouse.

flow. With manufacturers asking for payment and customers asking for extensions, the distributor can wind up feeling a bit squeezed at times.

The good news is that there are ways around it: by being judicious about your collections, thorough with your customer credit checks, and miserly when negotiating terms with suppliers. "Cash flow is a terribly important item, especially for new distributors," says John M. "For anyone whom you don't collect cash from, be sure to check out their credibility very carefully." He adds that of those you wish to check out, about 98 percent won't have a Dun & Bradstreet rating to access. "Particularly in rural areas, you just can't do it by D&B," he adds. "Instead, you'll have to inquire about them at the local bank. And ask the potential customer who else they do business with; then go and ask at those places, too."

On the other side of the equation, Kristi Tolman, vice president of corporate marketing for Pinacor Inc., a distributor of technology products in Tempe, Arizona, says that the real challenge for new distributors who want a positive cash flow involves setting up strong credit relationships with vendors. "You need these to be in place because in turn, you are then extending credit to your own customers," she says, adding that you not only need the financial relationships that allow you to purchase the product, but also those that allow you to extend credit to those customers who want to purchase from you. "For these reasons, establishing good credit relationships is something that needs to be done in the early stages of business."

Tax Issues to Consider

While there are few things that distributors need to do differently from any other business in terms of filing state and federal income taxes, sales tax is a sticky area of which every distributor must be aware.

When it comes to collecting sales tax, the real challenge lies in determining which of your customers are tax exempt and which are not. Generally, if your customer is reselling products to an end user, that customer is tax exempt. Schools and religious organizations are also usually tax exempt. However, you cannot take their word for it because ultimately, the responsibility will fall on your shoulders to collect from those who should be paying.

"You have some people who are tax exempt and some who are not, but if you neglect to collect from those who owe, then you will pay the back taxes plus a penalty from the Department of Revenue," explains John M. "Any number of people will tell you they are tax exempt, but you must have their tax-exempt form on file, and it must be signed and must include their tax-exempt number." He adds that while the distributor is responsible for collecting the appropriate forms, customers who falsify information are held accountable. The distributor is covered as long as the form is on file.

According to John, the key is to be "judicious about collecting your sales tax." The distributor who has the appropriate forms on file and collects from those without tax numbers will find itself in a good position if a sales tax audit rears its ugly head.

When figuring out the profitability of your new company, it's always handy to have the numbers in a chart format for easy access and comparison. The Atlanta-based Industrial Distribution Association (IDA) has broken that information down into two charts: a standard chart of accounts (see page 81), which lists most categories that a wholesale distributor uses, and a standard balance sheet (see page 82), which compares expenses vs. income to figure out your company's net worth. According to the IDA, distributors in need of more-detailed financial records can establish their own subgroupings within the listed categories.

In the last chapter, we'll give you some terrific tips and inspirational stories (and a few words of warning) from entrepreneurs who have already gotten their feet wet in the wholesale distribution business and who want to share their expertise with you.

Standard Chart of Accounts

The Industrial Distribution Association of Atlanta recommends using the following standard chart of operating accounts.

Goods Sold

1. Company sales: _____
   (including stock sales, special order sales, direct shipment sales, service shop sales, and returns and allowances)
2. Cost of goods sold: _____
   (including cost of stock sales, special order sales, direct shipment sales, and service sales)
3. Subtract line 2 from line 1: _____

Operating Expenses

4. Selling expenses: _____
   (includes outside sales and sales administration expenses, inside sales expenses, purchasing expenses, delivery expenses, land and building occupancy expenses, warehouse and service shop operating expenses, office expenses, administrative and general expenses, data processing expenses, labor expenses, and other expenses involved with running your company)

Other Income and Deductions

5. Other income: _____
   (includes cash discounts earned, commissions or rebates, income from investments, and miscellaneous income)
6. Other deductions: _____
   (includes cash discounts allowed, interest on borrowed money, loss on sales of capital assets, and loss from bad debts)

Net Profit Before Taxes

7. Add lines 3 and 5: _____
8. Add lines 4 and 6: _____
9. Subtract line 8 from line 7: _____
   (This is your company's net profit before taxes.)

Less Taxes on Income

10. Federal taxes on income: _____
11. State taxes on income: _____
12. Total income taxes: _____

Net Profit (or Loss) for the Year

13. Subtract line 12 from line 9: _____

▲

Standard Balance Sheet

The Industrial Distribution Association of Atlanta recommends using the following standard balance sheet to figure out your company's net worth:

Assets

All Current Assets	
Cash	
Accounts receivable	
Notes receivable	
Inventory (as reported on federal tax return)	
LIFO reserve	
Other current assets (including prepaid expenses such as catalog, insurance, interest)	
All Fixed Assets	
Real estate (appraisal or cost)	
Land	
Land improvements	
Building and improvements	
Machinery, furniture, vehicles, office equipment, etc.	
Other Fixed Assets	
Investments at cost or market	
Other assets	
Total Assets:	

Liabilities

All Current Liabilities	
Accounts payable	
Notes payable (include current portion of long-term debt and short-term bank loans)	
Federal and state income tax payable	
Payroll deductions	
Accrued expenses (salaries, commissions, sales taxes, payroll taxes, profit sharing, mortgage payable, etc.)	
Other current liabilities	
All Long-Term Liabilities	
Long-term debt (including mortgage)	
Total Liabilities (current and long-term):	
To figure your company's net worth, subtract liabilities from assets:	

Learning
from the Pros

Let's face it: Everyone wants to be successful, and there's nothing quite like starting your own business to enrich your life personally and financially. Sometimes, however, the road from start to finish is a bumpy one. The first two years of your wholesale distributorship's existence will be the "learning" years, when you experience the ups and downs of being a new business owner in a new industry.

On the positive side, plenty of wholesale distributors came before you and are now overflowing with advice and inspiration that will help you reach your own goals. Here are a few thoughts to keep you going through the start-up phase.

Managing the Credit Game

Because every wholesaler plays the middleman position between manufacturer and distributor, the real challenge lies in leveraging that position to your best advantage. While it may appear that you're powerless being stuck between the two, there's also a "glass is half-full" way to look at the relationship. As a wholesale distributor, it's up to you to make the other two businesses work in sync: You're helping the manufacturer get its products to market, and you are helping the customer obtain the products he or she needs to run a business.

While playing that important role, one of the major mistakes a wholesale distributor should avoid at all costs is the overextension of credit to customers. This tends to occur when one or more of your customers demands extended payment terms on their invoices, yet your manufacturers are demanding their own payment terms on the other end. You can avoid this by being diligent about checking credit references, meticulous when explaining your payment terms to new customers, and careful about not letting your receivables become too old or "aged."

The other part of the credit issue is the customer who buys too much and leaves you "overexposed" (meaning one particular customer owes too large a percentage of your receivables). You can avoid this by setting an appropriate credit limit up front, then reviewing the customer's account on a twice-yearly basis (or whatever time frame works best for you). Credit limits can then be increased based on the customer's payment history.

Clearing the Hurdles

In any business, the obstacles to success are many. Fortunately, we all learn from our mistakes, so each new challenge usually leaves entrepreneurs smarter and more seasoned. At the Downers Grove, Illinois-based fastener distributorship, Greg F. says one of the major challenges he has faced involved whether or not to extend credit to a customer. "In the beginning, I learned to be very cautious about whom I extended credit to. My industry (fasteners) is renowned for its slow payers, and everyone learns the hard way." The key, Greg says, is to watch your back and be very careful when selecting which customers will pay cash and which will be offered a credit account.

Greg adds that money management is another issue that distributors must get a handle on. "For any start-up, the biggest issue is managing the money that comes in," he says. "Once the loose cash starts floating around, it's very easy to spend it in the wrong place and not plan for the future."

Good Advice to Heed

In the business world, advice for start-ups is rampant but not always accurate. Also, not all of it applies across the board, so what's good for the wholesale distributor may not be so good for, say, the manufacturer of widgets. For this reason, we've distilled a few important tidbits of advice from the wholesale distributors and experts we interviewed for this book. Here's what they had to say:

"In wholesale distribution, customer service is the key," says Dave Spreen, branch manager for Tom Duffy Co., a Eureka, California, distributor of flooring materials. "This includes going the extra mile, solving problems with technical expertise, and developing personal relationships with customers. Wholesalers must stay ahead of the curve on new products, and should also offer training and sales seminars to customers as often as possible. Finally, the distributor must always keep and project a positive, proactive attitude."

John M. of the Lexington, Kentucky, distributorship says that wholesale distributors must be "hands on" with the products they're selling and must be willing to sacrifice an extraordinary amount of time and effort in the early stages of their new companies. "If they aren't ready to do that, then their chances of success are certainly going to be limited," he says. "As the wholesale distributorship becomes a more mature business, entrepreneurs will find themselves not having to put in quite that much energy, and will find that the business is not as dependent on them. One last note: I would advise all distributors to have a security system in place for their inventory, which can fly out the door if not properly safeguarded."

"New wholesale distributors must have some knowledge of their customer bases and of what they're selling," adds Mark Dierolf of Innovative Distribution Solutions in Gilbertsville, Pennsylvania. "The distributor who doesn't have a handle on these two issues when getting into the business is only fooling himself. Also, new entrepreneurs in the field should take advantage of the free resources out there: forming alliances, joining the chamber of commerce, and establishing relationships with bankers, to name a few. There are a lot of resources out there that are free for the taking."

Now that you have the soup-to-nuts view of what it takes to start a wholesale distribution business, we know you'll go out there and knock 'em dead. Be sure to check out this book's Appendix, which lists the phone numbers, addresses, and Web sites of important contacts, and the glossary for a view of industry-related terms you'll probably know by heart within a few months.

Good luck!

Appendix
Wholesale Distribution Resources

Getting your feet wet in a new industry can be daunting at times. For this reason, we suggest enlisting as much help as you can get (preferably free!) from industry organizations, business consultants who specialize in a particular field, and the vast number of books and other publications available on the market. Of course, the trick is to filter through and find out which of those resources can truly be of help and which ones can be a hindrance to your company's success.

While we couldn't list every available resource, we chose to concentrate on those that would most help the new wholesale distributor find business start-up assistance.

Associations and Professional Organizations

Alabama Wholesale Distributors Association, 600 Vestavia Pkwy., #220, Birmingham, AL 35216, (205) 823-8544, fax: (205) 823-5146

American Wholesale Marketers Association, 1128 16th St. NW, Washington, DC 20036-4808, (202) 463-2124, fax: (202) 463-6456, www.awma.org

California Distributors Association, 925 L St., #1100, Sacramento, CA 95814, (916) 446-7841, fax: (916) 442-5961

▲

Colorado Association of Distributors, 2150 W. 29th Ave., #200, Denver, CO 80211, (303) 443-4446, fax: (303) 458-0002

General Merchandise Distributors Council, 1275 Lake Plaza Dr., Colorado Springs, CO 80906, (719) 576-4260

Idaho Wholesale Marketers Association, Box 190716, Boise, ID 83719, (208) 375-5806, fax: (208) 375-4084

Industrial Distribution Association, 1277 Lenox Park Blvd., #275, Atlanta, GA 30329, (404) 266-8311, fax: (404) 266-3991, www.ida-assoc.org

Mississippi Wholesale Distributors Association, 11 Northtown Dr., #200B, Jackson, MS 39211, (601) 956-5787, fax: (601) 956-2887

National Association of Wholesaler-Distributors, 1725 K St. NW, Washington, DC 20006, (202) 872-0885, fax: (202) 785-0586, www.nawpubs.org, e-mail: pubs@nawd.org

North Carolina Wholesalers Association, P.O. Box 2021, Raleigh, NC 27602, (919) 831-4485, fax: (919) 834-8447

Southern Association of Wholesale Distributors, 1566 Kenzie Ct., #1001, Suwannee, GA 30024, (770) 418-2080, fax: (770) 418-0291, www.sawd.org

Texas Association of Wholesale Distributors, 7320 N. Mopac Expwy., #20, Austin, TX 78731-2309, (512) 346-6912, fax: (512) 346-6915

Virginia Wholesalers & Distributor Association, P.O. Box 2129, Richmond, VA 23218, (804) 643-4715, fax: (804) 649-0541

West Virginia Wholesalers Association, P.O. Box 1774, Huntington, WV 25718, (304) 529-1412, fax: (304) 529-3471

Books

Integrated Distribution Management: Competing on Customer Service, Time, and Cost, Christopher Gopal and Harold Cypress, Business One Irwin.

U.S. Industry and Trade Outlook (updated annually), The McGraw-Hill Companies and U.S. Department of Commerce/International Trade Association, 2 Penn Plaza, New York, NY 10121-2298, (212) 904-2786, www.mcgraw-hill.com

Managing Channels of Distribution, Kenneth Rolnicki, Amacom Books

The Complete Distribution Handbook, Timothy Van Mieghem, Prentice Hall

Wholesale Distribution Channels: New Insights and Perspectives, Bert Rosenbloom, Haworth Press

Consultants and Experts

The Infinity Group, Neil Gillespie, P.O. Box 15884, Pittsburgh, PA 15244, (412) 490-6950, www.infinitygrp.com, e-mail: ngillespie@infinitygrp.com

Innovative Distribution Solutions Inc., Mark Dierolf, 311 County Line Rd., Bldg. 16, Gilbertsville, PA 19525, (610) 473-7330, fax: (610) 473-7334, www.idsincusa.com

Pembroke Consulting Inc., Adam Fein, 1401 Walnut St., #620, Philadelphia, PA 19102, (215) 523-5700, fax: (215) 523-5758, www.pembroke-consulting.com

Pinacor Inc., Kristi Tolman, 3001 S. Priest Dr., Tempe, AZ 85283, (480) 366-7919, www.pinacor.com

Pyramid Products Inc., Paul Lineback, P.O. Box 2966, Spokane, WA 99220, (509) 252-2860, fax: (509) 252-2865, www.pyrprods.com, e-mail: info@pyrprods.com

Tom Duffy Co., Dave Spreen, 2223 Second St., Eureka, CA 95501, (707) 443-2231, www.tomduffy.com

Market Research

Industrial Market Information Inc., Rusty Duncan, 1313 Fifth St. SE, #208, Minneapolis, MN 55414, (612) 379-3939, fax: (612) 379-3875, www.imidata.com

Publications

Electronic Distribution Today, Custom Media Inc., P.O. Box 23069, Chagrin Falls, OH 44023, (440) 543-9451, fax: (440) 543-9764, www.edtmag.com, e-mail: edtmag@aol.com

Industrial Distribution, Cahners Publishing Co., 275 Washington St., Newton, MA 02158-1630, (617) 964-3030, fax: (617) 558-4327, www.inddist.com

Modern Distribution Management, P.O. Box 13507, Minneapolis, MN 55414, (612) 623-1074, www.mdm.com

Today's Distributor, Cygnus Publishing Inc., 1233 Janesville Ave., Fort Atkinson, WI 53538, (920) 563-6388, fax: (920) 563-1702, www.todaysdistributor.com

Software Publishers

Amplexus Corp., 201 Alameda Del Prado, #300, Novato, CA 94949, (415) 382-0111, fax: (415) 382-7929, www.amplexus.com

Eclipse Inc., 2 Enterprise Dr., #406, Shelton, CT 06484, (800) 9-ECLIPSE, www.eclipseinc.com

NxTrend, 5555 Tech Center Dr., #300, Colorado Springs, CO 80919-2309, (719) 590-8940, fax: (719) 528-1465, www.nxtrend.com, e-mail: info@nxtrend.com

Prophet 21 Inc., 19 West College Ave., Yardley, PA 19067, (800) PROPHET, www.distribution-software.net

Successful Wholesale Distributors

Borvin Beverage, Don Mikovch, 1022 King St., Alexandria, VA 22314, (703) 683-9463, fax: (703) 836-6654, www.borvinbeverage.com, e-mail: dmikovch@hotmail.com

Brock-McVey Co., John McDonald III, P.O. Box 55487, Lexington, KY 40555, (606) 355-1412, www.brockmcvey.com

Carver Industrial Products and E-Fastener Inc., Greg Fields, P.O. Box 409165, Downers Grove, IL 60640, (888) 236-3325, fax: (773) 645-6411, www.e-fastener.com, e-mail: info@efastener.com

Clark Security Products, Marshall Merrifield, 4775 Viewridge Ave., San Diego, CA 92014, (800) 241-3930, fax: (619) 974-5269, www.clarksecurity.com

OTP Sales Inc., Keith Schwartz, 1314 Lloyd Rd., Wickliffe, OH 44092, (440) 943-9933, fax: (440) 943-9944, e-mail: kds1@ mail.multiverse.com

Glossary

Alliance: an agreement in which two or more companies team up to increase their buying power or increase efficiencies within their firms.

Back-end activities: those activities that go on behind the scenes, such as warehouse setup and organization, shipping and receiving, customer service, etc.

Balance sheet: a financial statement used to report a company's total assets, liabilities, and equity.

Broker: someone who facilitates the transfer of materials between manufacturer and customer but generally doesn't hold inventory.

Build-out: modifying the interior of a location to meet your company's needs.

Business-to-business: a method of doing business in which a company sells to other companies and not to end users.

Consolidation: a trend in which companies either buy one another or merge with one another to increase efficiencies.

Cost per thousand (CPM): when buying advertising (media), this refers to the cost it takes to reach 1,000 people.

▲

Direct sales: when a manufacturer bypasses the distribution channel and sells directly to the end user.

Distribution channel: a way of distributing goods that finds products moving from manufacturer to distributor to end user.

Drop-ship: a shipping method in which a manufacturer ships directly to a distributor's customer.

Dun & Bradstreet: an agency that furnishes subscribers with market statistics and the credit ratings of companies.

Durable goods: products that can be used repeatedly (office equipment, furniture, etc.).

End user: the person or entity that will ultimately use a manufactured product.

Fill rate: the rate at which a company fills customer orders.

First in, first out (FIFO): an accounting system used to value inventory for tax purposes.

Free on board (FOB): a common shipping term that means the price of the goods covers transportation to the port of shipment and the usual loading charges.

GAF: general merchandise, apparel, and furniture.

GDP: gross domestic product, or the amount of goods produced in the United States each year.

Inventory: the amount of product that a distributor stores in a warehouse or other facility.

Lots: preferred quantities (usually large) of a certain product that a manufacturer wants to ship to a distributor or end user.

Markup: the amount of money a distributor adds to their cost before selling to their own customers.

Nondurable goods: products with a predetermined life span (writing paper, groceries, etc.).

Payment terms: the number days between the shipment of an item or items, and the date an invoice is due to be paid.

Profit & loss (P&L) statement: a worksheet that shows overall operating profit or loss for a company.

Rack merchandising: displaying products for sale on self-service display racks in retail stores.

Reseller: a company that buys product from a manufacturer and sells it to another company, who will then sell it to an end user.

Return on investment (ROI): a profitability measure used to gauge the earning power of the owner's total equity in the business.

Spread: the amount of money left over after a product has been sold and the vendor has been paid.

Standard industry classification (SIC): a method of classifying industries using definitions from the SIC manual.

Stock keeping unit (SKU): a term used to define each item stocked in a warehouse or store.

Supply chain: the product and information flow that encompasses all parties, beginning with a manufacturer's suppliers and ending with the end user.

Warehouse manager: the employee ultimately responsible for the smooth running of a distribution facility.

Index

Start-Up Guides
Books
Software

To order our catalog call 800-421-2300.
Or visit us online at smallbizbooks.com

Entrepreneur Magazine's
SmallBizBooks.com